"This lucid new translation of the an intoxicating, not to say spiritually inebriated, account of his search for union with God. An assiduous reader and translator of earlier contemplative texts, he blends together the languor of Richard Rolle, the apophatic austerity of the *Cloud*-author, the theological intensity of Heinrich Suso and the *devotio moderna*, and the liquefying ardour of Marguerite Porete. The resulting synthesis produces a new, urgently prophetic voice of meltingly eloquent spiritual longing existing in transcendent tension with the structures of his daily life as a Carthusian."

> —Vincent Gillespie
> J.R.R. Tolkien Professor of English
> University of Oxford

"This book makes available in modern English one of the most significant contributions to the contemplative tradition of fifteenth-century England. By fusing in such a sophisticated way the apophatic and the cataphatic approaches to the contemplative life as part of his experience, Methley's writings challenge our contemporary desire for categorization and division. The excellent translations by Barbara Newman bring to light the daily mystical experiences and the pastoral concerns of a Carthusian monk following a strict monastic life. Her notes and the outstanding general introduction by Laura Saetveit Miles provide a wealth of information about the rich religious tradition from which Methley's corpus emerged."

> —Denis Renevey
> Professor of Medieval English Language and Literature
> University of Lausanne

CISTERCIAN STUDIES SERIES: NUMBER TWO HUNDRED EIGHTY-SIX

The Works of Richard Methley

translated by Barbara Newman

with an introduction by Laura Saetveit Miles

α

Cistercian Publications
www.cistercianpublications.org

LITURGICAL PRESS
Collegeville, Minnesota
www.litpress.org

A Cistercian Publications title published by Liturgical Press

Cistercian Publications
Editorial Offices
161 Grosvenor Street
Athens, Ohio 45701
www.cistercianpublications.org

Translated from *The Works of Richard Methley*, vol. 1 of *Mount Grace Charterhouse and Late Medieval English Spirituality*, ed. John P. H. Clark and James Hogg, *Analecta Cartusiana* 64, no. 3 (2016); (Salzburg: Institut für Anglistik und Amerikanistik, 2017).

Biblical passages are translated from the Vulgate by Barbara Newman. All rights reserved.

1	2	3	4	5	6	7	8	9

Library of Congress Cataloging-in-Publication Data

Names: Methley, Richard, 1451- author. | Newman, Barbara, 1953- translator.
Title: The works of Richard Methley / translated by Barbara Newman ; with an
   introduction by Laura Saetveit Miles.
Description: Athens, Ohio : Cistercian Publications ; Collegeville, Minnesota :
   Liturgical Press, 2021. | Series: Cistercian studies series ; number two hundred
   eighty-six | Previously published as: vol. 1 of Mount Grace Charterhouse and
   Late Medieval English Spirituality, ed. John P. H. Clark and James Hogg,
   Analecta Cartusiana 64, no. 3 (2016); (Salzburg: Institut für Anglistik und
   Amerikanistik, 2017) | Includes bibliographical references and index. | Summary:
   "This book contains translations of Richard Methley's treatises dating from the
   1480s including a guide to contemplative prayer, a spiritual diary, and an
   unknown work on the discernment of spirits"— Provided by publisher.
Identifiers: LCCN 2020032652 (print) | LCCN 2020032653 (ebook) | ISBN
   9780879072865 (paperback) | ISBN 9780879076863 (epub) | ISBN
   9780879076863 (mobi) | ISBN 9780879076863 (pdf)
Subjects: LCSH: Theology—History—To 1500.
Classification: LCC BR100 .M4413 2021 (print) | LCC BR100 (ebook) | DDC
   248—dc23
LC record available at https://lccn.loc.gov/2020032652
LC ebook record available at https://lccn.loc.gov/2020032653

Contents

Introduction*

Richard Methley (ca. 1451–1527/28) was a Carthusian monk whose spiritual writings constitute a significant contribution to the Latin religious literature of late medieval England. Methley's three surviving mystical works intertwine the traditions of apophatic theology and affective spirituality with the genres of contemplative treatise and visionary account. He compared himself to the hermit and mystic Richard Rolle (d. 1349), and a contemporary later compared him to the laywoman and visionary Margery Kempe (d. after 1438). Few readers today, however, have heard of him, and even among specialists in medieval religion he is barely known. In this volume, his five surviving works are translated for the first time. Their obscurity—due in large part to their challenging Latin, the limited accessibility of modern editions, and the lack of translations until now—is undeserved. They offer a vivid view into the contemplative milieu of the Carthusian Order, and an engaging, idiosyncratic glimpse into the mystical experiences of a monk who felt driven to document those divine encounters for the benefit of his fellow Christians.

What little we know about Richard Methley can be gleaned mostly from the autobiographical aspects of his writings. He

* I would like to thank Barbara Newman, Michael Sargent, Katherine Zieman, Addison H. Hart, Antti Saarilahti, Kristin Saetveit, J. Duane Saetveit, and the Literature and Religion Research Group at the University of Bergen for their feedback on earlier drafts of this Introduction.

carefully dates his mystical experiences according to his age and the number of years since his profession as a monk, and his death is recorded in the obituaries from the Carthusian General Chapter for 1528 (and thus occurred sometime between spring 1527 and May 3, 1528).[1] He was born around 1451/52 to the Furth family in the village of Methley, just outside Leeds in Yorkshire. Whether or not he attended university or was ordained early on, he does not say, and no evidence survives. Nonetheless, he acquired ready fluency in Latin. A defining year in his life was 1476, when at the age of twenty-five he was professed as a monk at Mount Grace Charterhouse in North Yorkshire, where he would become vicar and live until his death around the age of seventy-seven. As he explains in *The Refectory of Salvation*, he was inspired to join the hermit-like Carthusian Order after visiting an "elderly recluse" or anchoress enclosed in a cell attached to a chapel, to whom he publicly gave a small donation while secretly giving much more. Against his wishes the recluse's servant revealed his generosity, for which he received both praise and censure from others. Upon the recluse's death a few days later, he too was led within three months "to a solitary cell to live there as a Carthusian" (chap. 20).

The Carthusians

At Mount Grace, Methley joined the Carthusians' life of contemplation as it had been practiced nearly unchanged for almost four hundred years, ever since the foundation of the Grande Chartreuse by Bruno of Cologne in the Chartreuse Mountains of France (1084). The Carthusian Order, still vibrant today, is unique in that it functions as a community of solitaries or hermits. In the isolation of their individual cells, more like small apartments set around a

---

1. Michael Sargent, "Richard Methley," *Oxford Dictionary of National Biography* (Oxford: Oxford University Press, 2004): https://doi.org/10.1093/ref:odnb/69525. For Methley's obituary, see *The Chartae of the Carthusian General Chapter: MS. Parkminster B.62 (1504–1513)*, vol. 1, ed. John Clark, *Analecta Cartusiana* (1992): 28, lines 16–17.

cloister, and nearly self-sufficient with back gardens, monks spend most of their week alone: they eat, sleep, read, and pray by themselves, performing almost all of the Divine Office in private. They gather communally for Vespers and Matins (the evening and night Offices), on Sundays and significant holy days for Mass and lunch in the refectory, and for chapter meetings.[2] This daily and annual rhythm of private prayer and public liturgy shaped Methley's life and oeuvre, and is especially evident in *The Refectory of Salvation*. Carthusian monks also wrote or copied manuscripts in the private scriptorium part of their cell, facilitating the "literary character of the spirituality of the Carthusian Order," in the words of Michael Sargent.[3] Book production has always been a central part of their vocation; they were not allowed to preach publicly. Guigo I (d. 1136), fifth prior of the Grande Chartreuse, encapsulated this priority in his statutes for the Order, the *Consuetudines*: "We wish books to be made with the greatest attention and guarded most carefully, as eternal food for our souls, so that because we cannot preach the word of God by our mouths, we may do so with our hands."[4] As scribes, Carthusians copied thousands of manuscripts of Christian theology, spirituality, and history, thus promoting the preservation and circulation of an enormous ancient and medieval tradition. They also composed and copied their own texts—as Methley did. In many ways the Carthusian focus on books brought individual solitaries out of their cells into networks of communities of varying scales. Voices like Methley's could address local,

---

2. Richard W. Pfaff, "Liturgy at the English Charterhouses," in *The Liturgy in Medieval England: A History* (Cambridge: Cambridge University Press, 2009), 265.

3. Michael Sargent, "The Transmission by the English Carthusians of Some Late Medieval Spiritual Writings," *Journal of Ecclesiastical History* 27 (1976): 225–40, at 240.

4. Guigo I, *Consuetudines* XXVIII.3, from *Coutumes de Chartreuse*, ed. Maurice Laporte (Paris: Éditions du Cerf, 1984), trans. in Jessica Brantley, *Reading in the Wilderness: Private Devotion and Public Performance in Late Medieval England* (Chicago: University of Chicago Press, 2007), 334, n. 73. See 27–57 for a brief history of the Carthusian Order in general and in England, their book culture, and the context of this oft-discussed quotation.

national, and international readerships, and copying manuscripts for exchange could link together different reading circles, primarily monastic, but also secular and lay.

The Carthusian Order soon spread across the Channel and exerted an influence in England similar to what it had on the Continent. Witham Charterhouse was founded in 1178, followed by seven others, including London in 1370, Mount Grace in 1398, and Sheen in 1414. Carthusians made large contributions to the production and circulation of religious literature in medieval England. Through gifts, copying, and composition, they grew vast libraries of devotional and spiritual works, often of quite imaginative literary genres at the forefront of nascent trends, and they fostered very specialized vernacular mysticism in addition to Latin.[5] In particular, the Carthusians had a high regard for medieval women visionaries, and they played a major role in the preservation of English copies of texts by Elisabeth of Schönau, Mechthild of Hackeborn, Marguerite Porete, Birgitta of Sweden, Catherine of Siena, and Englishwomen Julian of Norwich and Margery Kempe. To what extent they disseminated such works beyond the charterhouse walls is more debatable, and is an issue taken up below in reference to Methley's connections to both Porete and Kempe. Regardless, as a literary and spiritual force, the order remained a significant part of English religious culture until the Dissolution of the Monasteries in 1538, just ten years after Methley's death.

Methley's Works

During his enclosure of over half a century, Methley was a prolific author of his own religious texts as well as a translator and glossator of texts originally composed in Middle English. His four

---

5. Brantley, *Reading in the Wilderness*, 57. See also E. Margaret Thompson, *The Carthusian Order in England* (London: Society for Promoting Christian Knowledge, 1930).

extant original compositions in Latin and one in the vernacular are translated here; they represent perhaps half his total output as an author, as he identifies four other Latin texts that do not seem to have survived. And there were evidently more: in *The Bedroom of the beloved Beloved*, one of his earlier surviving texts, he refers to "the many books I have already written" (chap. 1). An approximate timeline for his known corpus, and when his documented mystical experiences occurred, can be extrapolated from their internal evidence (works marked with an * are translated in this volume):

1484 *Scola amoris languidi* * (*The School of Languishing Love*), a treatise on contemplative prayer including references to mystical experiences on August 6 of that year;

1484 *Cellarium* (*The Cellar*) does not survive but is mentioned in chapter 30 of *The Bedroom* as being written in the previous year;

1485 *Dormitorium dilecti Dilecti* * (*The Bedroom of the beloved Beloved*) records mystical experiences in April of that year;

1486/87? *De Marie nomine et sacramento altaris* (*On the Name of Mary and the Sacrament of the Altar*) does not survive but is mentioned in chapters 32 and 35 of *The Refectory;*

1487/88 *Trivium excellencie* (*Three Ways of Excellence*) does not survive but is mentioned in chapter 34 of *The Refectory of Salvation* as having been begun on December 8, 1487;

1487 *Refectorium salutis* * (*The Refectory of Salvation*) records mystical experiences between October 6 and December 13 of that year;

1491   *Speculum animarum simplicium*, a glossed translation into Latin of the Middle English version of *The Mirror of Simple Souls* by Marguerite Porete;

1491   *Divina caligo ignoranciae*, a glossed translation into Latin of the Middle English treatise *The Cloud of Unknowing*.

Other texts are of unknown date but probably from later in his life:

Defensorium solitarie sive contemplative vite (*A Defense of the Solitary or Contemplative Life*) does not survive but is mentioned in chapter 23 of *The Experience of Truth* as having already been written;

Experimentum veritatis* (*The Experience of Truth*), a treatise on the discernment of spirits, survives only partially;

To Hugh Hermit: An Epistle of Solitary Life Nowadays*, a letter of spiritual counsel in the vernacular to a nearby hermit.

It appears that Methley was forgotten after the Reformation until just a few decades ago. Almost all of the impetus behind bringing Methley's life and works to modern readers can be ascribed to the Carthusian scholar James Hogg (d. 2018). By means of the *Analecta Cartusiana* series begun in the late 1970s, Hogg published diplomatic transcriptions and editions of the surviving texts; *Experience* was edited by Michael Sargent. In 2017 Hogg and John Clark co-edited an updated volume of Methley's complete corpus, and the present translation is based on this edition, with consultation of the medieval manuscripts.[6]

---

6. *The Works of Richard Methley*, vol. 1 of *Mount Grace Charterhouse and Late Medieval English Spirituality*, ed. John P. H. Clark and James Hogg, *Analecta Cartusiana* 64, no. 3 (2016); (Salzburg: Institut für Anglistik und Amerikanistik, 2017).

The Manuscripts

In contrast to better-known authors like Bernard of Clairvaux, whose writings were widely copied and circulated in the medieval period, the works of Richard Methley come down to us today only in single manuscript witnesses. These material artifacts reveal important information about their texts' meaning, reception, and contemporary significance. *School*, *Bedroom*, and *Refectory* are preserved in Cambridge, Trinity College MS O.2.56, a manuscript that shows that these texts were well regarded by multiple scribes and readers, who made special efforts to improve their quality and accessibility to a monastic audience. In contrast, we learn less about *The Experience of Truth* and *To Hugh Hermit* from their copies in London, Public Record Office Collection SP 1/239. We know neither why they were copied nor who might actually have read them.

Cambridge, Trinity College MS O.2.56 functions as a unique anthology of Methley's mystical texts. It contains five items in total:

1. fols. 1^r–21^r *The School of Languishing Love*

2. fols. 21^v–22^r Latin hymn and collect for the Name of Jesus and the Five Wounds (translated in the present volume at the end of *The School*)

   fol. 23^r–24^v stubs

3. fols. 25^r–48^r *The Bedroom of the beloved Beloved*
   fol. 48^v blank

4. fols. 49^r–70^v *The Refectory of Salvation*
   fol. 71^{rv} blank

5. fols. 72^r–75^v Table of contents

The Trinity manuscript can be dated to the late fifteenth century on paleographical grounds; it was probably copied and read at an English monastery or charterhouse with close connection to Methley, if not at Mount Grace itself.[7] A first and second main section of the paper manuscript can be distinguished in several ways: different scribes, similar but differing watermarks and thus similar but not identical paper, a lower position of the text-block and a lack of ruling in the second section, and telltale stubs between the sections showing that empty folios were cut out when the sections were brought together. There are several hands in the manuscript, showing that it was made over some time and carefully read and corrected by at least three different scribes. The first main scribe, Hand A, wrote the first section (fols. 1–22), and the second main scribe, Hand B, wrote the second section (fols. 25–76).

Nicholas Bell suggests the following order of events in the manuscript's construction: first, Hand A writes fols. 1–22, including marginal notations. Second, a different hand adds marginal notes on fols. 4^v, 5^r, 5^v, and 19^v, and foliates fols. 1–24. Third, Hand B writes fols. 25–76 on new paper stock (also writing folio numbers and catch words), and adds annotations to fols. 5^r–11^r, 18^r, and 22^r. Finally, the blank folios 23–24 are removed when the two sections are bound together.[8] At some point, yet another hand adds notes on fols. 6^r, 21^v, and 22^v. These details show that the manuscript was subject to annotation and correction throughout its production and afterward, with fairly frequent erasures and interlinear insertions.

---

7. For a full description, see printed catalogue entry 1160 in M. R. James, *The Western Manuscripts in the Library of Trinity College, Cambridge*, vol. 3 (Cambridge: Cambridge University Press, 1902), 176–78; also Clark and Hogg, *The Works*, viii–ix. The manuscript is available online as of this writing.

8. See Nicholas Bell's description of the manuscript in Clark and Hogg, *The Works*, ix.

As usual, these scribes did not sign their work, but it seems likely that they were monks, maybe also at Mount Grace. Could Methley himself have been one of the scribes of the Trinity manuscript, as M. R. James has suggested?[9] This is almost certainly not the case for several reasons. As Hogg and Clark note, none of the hands matches Methley's autograph, captured in a brief letter in the vernacular that he wrote to Henry, Lord Clifford (d. 1523), who was a patron of Mount Grace and endowed new cells.[10] In addition, the colophon of *Refectory* refers to the author in the third person in a way suggesting that Methley was not the scribe at least for the second section of the manuscript:[11] "Here ends *The Refectory of Salvation*, composed from the most opulent drunkenness by that man of God, Richard Methley, filled with delights." Finally, as noted in the Translator's Preface below, the texts themselves contain grammatical and other errors that would seem to preclude the author himself from having been the copyist. What quality of source material these scribes had, how distanced they were from Methley's autographs, and how closely he may or may not have been involved in correcting this manuscript is difficult to tell.

The fact that so many scribes interacted with this anthology, copying the different texts and annotating and correcting them, shows that Methley's works were valued and that extensive efforts were made to increase their reliability. Carthusians in general were very concerned with correcting texts to ensure the textual uniformity of books and the integrity of the individual copy, and to prevent that copy from perpetuating errors when it was copied again. We can assume that the monks who worked on the Trinity

9. James, *The Western Manuscripts*, 176.

10. The letter is preserved in London, British Library Add. MS 48965, fol. 10^r, and is reproduced on a small scale in Clark and Hogg, *The Works*, xii. An edited transcription of the letters to Lord Clifford in MS 48965 can be found in A. G. Dickens, ed., *The Clifford Letters of the Sixteenth Century*, Surtees Society 172 (Durham: University of Durham, 1957), 62–74.

11. Clark and Hogg, *The Works*, viii.

manuscript expected it to be an exemplar for further copies, though none of those survive today. While the Trinity manuscript presents versions of *School*, *Bedroom*, and *Refectory* with some linguistic errors and corrupted passages that pose a challenge, the material evidence of the manuscript suggests that its creators tried hard to present texts of as high a quality as possible because they thought they were worth reading and reproducing.

Other evidence in the Trinity manuscript also reveals interesting information about both how different monastic readers accessed the texts and how the texts were made accessible to them. For instance, seven parchment tabs, much like a medieval version of our modern Post-its, are still glued to the outer edges of seven folios.[12] Such tabbing was a typical practice in medieval book production and can be found in other Carthusian manuscripts. The tabs indicate that readers wanted to mark certain places in the text for frequent later reference. Hand B also went to the trouble to add at the end of the manuscript a comprehensive table of contents listing the title of every chapter in each of the three works. Another major effort toward accessibility is the inclusion of nearly ninety marginal glosses, short explanatory annotations (much like commentary notes in a modern textbook), to accompany *The School of Languishing Love*. Almost all were copied by the same scribe as the text itself, with a few others added by the other main scribe.[13] (We have included translations of all glosses in the footnotes; they are also included in the Latin edition.) In many ways, these marginalia function as an official paratextual apparatus and should be considered integral to the main work itself.

Generally, the glosses are explanatory and didactic, clarifying the meaning of specific words or theological terms, supplementing

12. Tabs are still attached to the outer edges of fol. 12 (*School*, opening of chap. 13), fol. 21 (*School*, opening of chap. 24), fol. 27 (*Bedroom*, opening of chap. 4), fol. 32 (*Bedroom*, chaps. 14–15), fol. 44 (*Bedroom*, chaps. 31–32), fol. 50 (*Refectory*, opening of chap. 2), and fol. 65 (*Refectory*, chap. 31).

13. One other explanatory gloss in the manuscript can be found in chap. 6 of *Refectory*.

a line with a scriptural verse, or simply expanding on the main text with more clarity. They illuminate aspects the expected readership might have struggled with, and sometimes they add another interpretive layer helping the reader to understand the text in a deeper or more sophisticated way. Methley almost certainly composed these glosses himself for his fellow monks; in that respect they offer a reliable and coherent part of *School*. Two notes suggest Methley as self-glossator because they feature the first person, seeming to refer to the main work and not just the glosses. These are the notes in chapter 13 ("as I said before") and the beginning of chapter 22 ("As I have explained above"). Methley also glossed his Latin translations of two difficult mystical works, *The Cloud of Unknowing* and Marguerite Porete's *The Mirror of Simple Souls*, with similar explanatory and interpretive aims, though also with a keen awareness of the potential heterodoxy of those texts—especially *The Mirror*.

The other two texts are preserved in a different way, with less information about their scribes and readers. London, Public Record Office Collection SP 1/239 preserves the second half of Methley's treatise on the discernment of spirits, *The Experience of Truth* (fols. 262^r–265^v), and his letter of guidance to a hermit, *To Hugh Hermit* (fols. 266^r–267^v). This manuscript is not so much a standard bound codex as a collection of individually mounted letters, including some others related to the Carthusians (fols. 156–162; 184).[14] Methley's pieces are both copied by the same scribe in the early sixteenth century. Unlike the Trinity manuscript, these copies show only corrections by the main scribe and no marks or marginalia left by other readers, so it is unclear how broad a circulation they received. Their origins and reading history are difficult to deduce, especially since they are small parts of a collection compiled later on. We could probably safely assume

---

14. These letters are detailed in Clark and Hogg, *The Works*, x, and James Hogg, "Carthusian Materials in London, Public Record Office Collection SP I/239," *Analecta Cartusiana* 37 (1977): 134–44.

they were copied and read by fellow Carthusians, as evidence suggests for the Trinity manuscript, but in fact even this much is unknown—as well as who or how many people actually read these texts. For instance, while Methley clearly wrote *To Hugh Hermit* expecting Hugh to receive a copy (and perhaps also hoping for wider dissemination), on the evidence of the single surviving witness, we might never know whether this letter reached any readers beyond the person who copied it.

The Spiritual Treatises: *School*, *Bedroom*, and *Refectory*

The three long treatises, *School*, *Bedroom*, and *Refectory*, all refer several times to readers as "my brothers." These were written for the benefit of a Carthusian audience with a solid foundation in text- and image-based meditation, who were now ready for the next level of contemplation, which moves beyond words and images.[15] The overall purpose of *School* is to give Methley's fellow monks a basic understanding of union with the divine and teach them how to approach it through contemplative practice. While in *School* his own mystical experience only comes up briefly, in *Bedroom* Methley shifts the balance to focus on his many kinds of spiritual illumination as models for the reader's advancement. Finally, *Refectory* moves toward full documentation of Methley's mystical experiences, in the form of a day-by-day (sometimes minute-by-minute) spiritual diary. What unites all three works is their shared rhetorical and thematic trope of a recurring refrain, a short phrase chosen from the Song of Songs—that endlessly fruitful erotic and allegorical scriptural text fueling so much mystical literature in the medieval tradition.[16]

15. For a brief account of Methley's mysticism, see Bernard McGinn, *The Varieties of Vernacular Mysticism, 1350–1550* (New York: Crossroad, 2012), 488–90.

16. On this tradition see Denys Turner, *Eros and Allegory: Medieval Exegesis of the Song of Songs,* CS 156 (Kalamazoo, MI: Cistercian Publications, 1995).

The refrain for *The School of Languishing Love* is from Song of Songs 2:5, *amore langueo*: "I languish for love." For Methley this phrase captures the contradiction of the contemplative's love for God and desire to be united with him, but being denied full dissolution in the Godhead while still living on earth. Simultaneously, it expresses God's pleasure and pain in loving sinful humans. Over twenty-four chapters, Methley sets out twelve different ways to understand how both people and God languish in love, as the basis for an approach to contemplation. He speaks directly to the reader, expounding the meaning and implications of languishing for love. Sometimes he ventriloquizes God himself at length, having God speak to the reader, as in chapter 5, "A disputation and complaint of God against ungrateful humanity." He cites his own experience of rapture in church at one point (chap. 7) to give a concrete example of the ineffability of the languor of love, while acknowledging the paradox of such an attempt. By chapter 16, he judges the reader informed enough to actually attempt meditation. He gives quite practical guidance: find a suitable place, sit in a soft seat, set a cross in front, and then direct the mind to God—for fifteen minutes, three times a day.[17] (The fact that Methley takes for granted that his readers had the time and space to follow this regimen reminds us that he had exclusively fellow monks in mind.) He goes so far as to include sample prayers for beginning and ending each session. The clear, explanatory glosses in the margin of the main text (translated here as footnotes) underline the way *School* aims to educate the reader in crucial aspects of prayer as an approach to its more advanced, mystical levels.

For monks past these beginning stages, *The Bedroom of the beloved Beloved* is less about praxis and more about the nature of

---

17. This practice, grounded in *The Cloud of Unknowing*, was popularized for lay use in the 1970s under the name of Centering Prayer and is still widely used. See Thomas Merton, *Contemplative Prayer* (New York: Herder and Herder, 1969), and Thomas Keating, *Foundations for Centering Prayer and the Christian Contemplative Life* (New York: Continuum, 2002).

ecstatic union itself. The refrain here is Song of Songs 5:2, *Ego dormio, et cor meum vigilat*: "I sleep and my heart is awake." Methley interprets this sentence in a variety of ways, centrally as being "awake in the love of God, asleep to the love of the world," in that "sleeping means taking no pleasure; being awake means taking pleasure," whether in God or in the world (chap. 8). In moving away from the didacticism of *School*, *Bedroom* directly addresses the connection between Methley's mystical experiences and their channeling into a text. From the start, and continuing throughout, he slips easily between addressing the reader and addressing God, beginning when he describes the composition of *Bedroom*: "in this book you [God] want me to write with you in a new mode of speaking, a most truthful mode. Sometimes this will be through inspiration, though differently than before. At other times it will be in dialogue, as in the many books I have already written through you" (chap. 1). (*School* and the lost work *The Cellar* are among those "many books"; the rest remain unknown.) At the same time we get a hint of the divine impetus behind Methley's drive to compose all the works. He quotes God as saying to him, "In this volume of yours, write all the words I speak to you" (chap. 1).

In order to elucidate this state of sleeping wakefulness, over the next thirty-six chapters Methley interweaves different analogies of divine love and union, interactive dialogue with Christ or God, and the description of a variety of his ecstatic experiences. He was ravished into "a marvelous light" while he was walking outdoors on Easter Day, 1485, as described in chapter 11; later on in chapter 23 he describes repeated, frequent ecstasies when God "ravished me above myself in the spirit" three or four times in an hour; and by chapter 31, he attests to having "peace not just for a moment, as scoffers say, but constantly." He also writes of several illuminations involving "spiritual visions," aligned with Augustine's category wherein "the soul is raptured into things seen that are similar to bodies, but are beheld in the spirit in such a way that the soul is totally removed from the bodily senses, more than in sleep but less than in death."[18] He sees Christ standing on top of a very high mountain (chap. 33), as well as two visions of the Virgin Mary acting as intercessor before Christ on his behalf (chaps. 22 and 36).

The last treatise, *The Refectory of Salvation*, completes the shift from contemplative instruction to spiritual autobiography and is devoted to relaying Methley's visionary and mystical experiences over approximately three months of 1487, from October 6 to mid-December. Here the scriptural refrain expresses the inebriation of spiritual illumination, from Song of Songs 5:1: "I have eaten my honeycomb with my honey, I have drunk my wine with my milk." Over forty-one chapters he details the ways in which he is "re-freshed by heavenly food": frequent raptures at all times and places, marked by heavenly song, spiritual illuminations or visions, bodily incapacitation, and vocal exclamations. Methley structures the text as a diary documenting these mystical experiences as happening with some regularity every few days, or even multiple times over a few hours. He identifies the day on which they occurred, usually in reference to a saint's feast or other holy day, and when they occur during the daytime, he mentions the relevant hour of the Divine Office or the Mass. The raptures sometimes overtake him during private prayer, but often happen unexpectedly in the middle of communal worship or even interrupt mundane activities such as making the bed. Methley shares these experiences with his "dearest brothers" by means of this book as an act of charity, interspersing his accounts of the mystical experiences with reflection on their import and theological context in a way he imagines will be helpful for his readers.

18. Augustine on the three forms of vision, *Literal Commentary on Genesis,* 12.26.53; trans. in *The Essential Writings of Christian Mysticism*, ed. Bernard McGinn (New York: Modern Library, 2006), 322.

The Spiritual Treatises: Sources and Traditions

As these three treatises increasingly rely on Methley's own contemplative experience and the authority of his union with the
divine, they make few explicit references to other works besides
Scripture, and they very rarely cite established authorities. Methley is well aware of how little he displays his learning. In *Bedroom*, he speaks to Christ but seems to address the concerns of
his readers when he comments, "Let our talk be about love, which
dwells freely in lovers and always gives a writer new material. . . . That is why those who discuss perceptible love rarely
scrutinize the words of others or cite standard authorities. Nor
do they organize their writings in the usual way, setting up divisions and subdivisions" (chap. 32). Authentic mystical experience, Methley insists, overrides any need to bow to a textual
tradition, through either writing style or citations. Indeed, a re-
sistance to the over-organization and over-citation of systematic
scholastic theology emerges in his works as a marker of the authenticity of his mystical accounts, a feature shared with some
other visionary texts such as *The Book of Margery Kempe*. Be
that as it may, however, these texts still show how Methley was
steeped in the interconnected traditions of affective piety, visionary literature, Rollean mysticism, Carthusian contemplative spirituality, and apophatic theology. That is the crucible out of which
these three spiritual treatises emerge.

Affective piety was a widespread and heterogeneous kind of
late-medieval spirituality marked by extreme emotionalism, devotion to the manhood and body of Christ, and vivid visualization
of biblical scenes as a form of prayer—all undergirded by a
"greater emphasis on self-examination, the inner emotions, and
the cultivation of an interior life."[19] By the late fifteenth century,

---

19. Anne Clark Bartlett and Thomas H. Bestul, "Introduction," in *Cultures of Piety:
Medieval English Devotional Literature in Translation* (Ithaca, NY: Cornell Univer-
sity Press, 1999), 2. See also the erudite and balanced overview of affective piety on
Wikipedia: https://en.wikipedia.org/wiki/Affective_piety.

when Methley was writing, this tradition had been developing over several hundred years through the influence of works by Cistercians such as Bernard of Clairvaux (d. 1153) and Aelred of Rievaulx (d. 1167), Franciscans like Saint Francis of Assisi (d. 1226) and Bonaventure (d. 1274), and, in the fourteenth century, the ever-popular pseudo-Bonaventuran text *Meditationes vitae Christi*. Among its countless vernacular adaptations, this descriptive Gospel meditation on Christ's life was transformed into a new Middle English version, *Mirror of the Blessed Life of Jesus Christ*, by Methley's fellow Carthusian, Nicholas Love (d. 1424), monk and prior of Mount Grace. The tradition of imaginatively participating in scenes of Christ's life likewise influenced the late medieval *Devotio Moderna* or Modern Devout movement in the Low Countries, a lay effort at religious reform known for its methodical approaches to prayer. Out of this movement came the influential text *The Imitation of Christ* by Thomas à Kempis (d. 1471), a Brother of the Common Life. Methley could well have been acquainted with the systematic meditation methods of the Modern Devout, as well as their textual practice of creating *rapiaria*, wherein "they copied out favorite passages encountered in their reading, or made notes to themselves, yielding over time a diary of religious reflections or a program of spiritual exercises."[20] Such a document recalls the structure of *Refectory*, though Methley's text resembles more a visionary log than a commonplace book.

In terms of his relationship with affective spirituality, Methley was not so much concerned with mentally recollecting the Bible as part of his spiritual practice. Rather, he was highly focused on the emotions and sensible perceptions elicited by imagining an intimate mystical relationship with Christ as expressed through metaphors of romantic love, a hallmark of affective piety. A specific example of one author's influence on Methley in the affective piety tradition is Henry Suso (d. 1366), a Dominican friar from Germany.

---

20. John Van Engen, *Sisters and Brothers of the Common Life: The Devotio Moderna and the World of the Later Middle Ages* (Philadelphia: University of Pennsylvania Press, 2008), 278. I would like to thank Katherine Zieman for this tip.

Suso's devotional masterpiece *Horologium Sapientiae* (*The Clock of Wisdom*) seems to have inspired Methley at least twice, though he does not name Suso explicitly. In *School*, chapter 21, Christ is lover as both male Bridegroom and female Eternal Wisdom, just as in *Horologium*; in *Bedroom*, chapter 16, the premise of the debate with a theologian draws on Suso. The English Carthusians were generally interested in Suso: a partial Middle English translation of *Horologium*, *The Treatise of the Seven Points of True Love and Everlasting Wisdom*, probably originated at Mount Grace, and it is cited in other Carthusian compilations.[21]

Hand in hand with these texts of affective piety went visionary literature in its various genres—either embedded in hagiography or as stand-alone revelatory accounts. If manuscripts linked to his house (or available through the Carthusian network) are any indication, Methley had access to one of England's best collections (if not its best collection) of medieval visionary women's texts. The Carthusian author of *A Mirror for Devout People* (ca. 1420–1440), for instance, frequently and approvingly cites by name "some revelations of approved women": continental holy women Elizabeth of Hungary (d. 1231), Mechthild of Hackeborn (d. 1298), Birgitta of Sweden (d. 1373), and Catherine of Siena (d. 1380).[22] In addition, the texts of native female visionaries Julian of Norwich (d. after 1416) and Margery Kempe (d. after 1438) were transmitted by the Carthusians and held at Methley's own house of Mount Grace. How much Methley had read these women-authored works or was influenced by them remains tantalizingly unclear and deserves further study. There is at least one likely point of overlap with Mechthild's *Liber specialis gratiae* (*Book of Special Grace*) in a vision at the end of *School* in chapter 33, and a few moments of similarity with Julian's writings, but per-

21. Dirk Schultze, "Wisdom in the Margins: Text and Paratext in *The Seven Points of True Love and Everlasting Wisdom*," *Études Anglaises* 66, no. 3 (2013): 341–56.

22. Paul J. Patterson, ed., *A Mirror to Devout People* (*Speculum devotorum*), EETS o.s. 346 (Oxford: Oxford University Press, 2016); discussion in the Introduction, xl–xliv, and mention in the text, 6, lines 125–26.

haps not enough to prove direct influence. Other Carthusians certainly saw close correlations between Methley and Kempe, as is explained below, but we hear nothing from Methley himself about Kempe or her *Book*.

Beyond quotations and rhetorical allusions to Scripture, which permeate all his writings, Methley names only one source directly: insular mystical writer Richard Rolle (d. 1349), hermit of Hampole. Like other English Carthusians, Methley admired Rolle, the "holy hermit" of the previous century, for his ecstatic experiences and solitary lifestyle, and read his large corpus of texts carefully. Rolle was born around 1300 in Yorkshire, not far from Mount Grace, and within his lifetime became well known as a mystic, author, and hermit, never formally professing as a monk or anchorite. When he died in 1349 he was involved with the Cistercian nunnery at Hampole and had written some vernacular texts for enclosed women there and elsewhere. By the time Methley was born about a hundred years later, Rolle had become one of England's most popular native authors of religious writing (though not without his detractors).[23] The Carthusians copied and preserved his many works, especially those that concern Rolle's ecstatic experiences and his approaches to the contemplative life.[24] *School*, *Bedroom*, and *Refectory* all show the influence of Rolle's *Incendium amoris* (*The Fire of Love*), *Emendatio vitae* (*The Amending of Life*), *Melos amoris* (*The Melody of Love*), *Ego dormio* (*I Sleep*), and possibly *The Commandment* and *The Form of Living*.

Methley openly relies on Rolle's influential vocabulary for expressing spiritual sensations in terms of love, languor, sweetness,

23. These detractors, including at least one Carthusian, seem to have been mostly concerned with Rolle's followers misinterpreting his teaching, rather than Rolle himself; see Michael Sargent, "Contemporary Criticism of Richard Rolle," *Analecta Cartusiana* 55, no. 1 (1985): 160–205.

24. On Carthusian manuscripts of Rolle, see Katherine Zieman, "Monasticism and the Public Contemplative in Late Medieval England: Richard Methley and His Spiritual Formation," *Journal of Medieval and Early Modern Studies* 42 (2012): 699–724, at 705.

warmth, and song (*amor, languor, dulcor, fervor, canor*), and many of these instances are identified in the notes to the translated texts. In *Refectory* he goes so far as to explicitly acknowledge his indebtedness to and yet distinction from his predecessor: "For my life consists of love, languor, sweetness, warmth, and song, yet perceptible warmth is the rarest. The Beloved has promised me that I would experience love more often in languor, just as the kindly Richard of Hampole experienced it more often in warmth. I have not read that he experienced such frequent languor" (chap. 12). Methley's distinction between the two mystics' differing experiences can be seen in their choices of title: Rolle's *fervor* is captured in the autobiographical *Incendium amoris* (*The Fire of Love*), and Methley's languor in *The School of Languishing Love*. It is remarkable that in this passage Methley not only compares his spiritual sensations to Rolle's, using Rolle's descriptors, but also uses these descriptors to explain Christ's promise of future mystical experience. In other words, Christ himself employs the vocabulary provided by Rolle. Barbara Newman's translation of *almus* as "kindly" captures Methley's sense of Rolle as one of his own "kind," a kindred soul leading a solitary life while also driven to document his mystical experiences. But *almus* also has a primary sense of "nourishing." Reading Rolle offers Methley a fertile source of language and rhetoric that helps nurture the textual engendering of his own divine encounters.

This formal influence can be seen in the frequent alliteration and internal rhyme found especially throughout *School*, but also in *Refectory* and *Bedroom* (as noted in the footnotes). Rolle's *Melos amoris* (*Melody of Love*), a "singularly virtuosic mystical text" that is "full of autobiographical glimpses and spiritual rhapsodies," as Andrew Albin observes, undoubtedly provided the most direct model for shaping Methley's Latin prose into an alliterative, lyrical literary language.[25] Methley likewise follows in

25. Andrew Albin, "Listening for *Canor* in Richard Rolle's *Melos Amoris*," in *Voice and Voicelessness in Medieval Europe*, ed. Irit Ruth Kleiman (New York: Palgrave, 2015), 177–97; *Richard Rolle's* Melody of Love*: A Study and Translation*

Rolle's footsteps in finding inspiration in the Song of Songs, a central text in many of Rolle's works. For instance, the refrain of *Bedroom*, "I sleep and my heart is awake" (Song 5:2), also supplies the title of one of Rolle's works, *Ego dormio* (*I Sleep*). This letter to a female recipient touches on angels, degrees of love, the spiritual life, and praying to Christ through the poetic songs it includes—all topics also of concern to Methley.

In fact, the songs Rolle includes in *Ego dormio*, as well as his large corpus of verse lyrics, strongly recall the poem titled "A devout prayer on the name of Jesus and the five wounds" included in the Trinity manuscript, between *School* and *Bedroom*. In light of Methley's imitation of Rolle as author and mystic, it would make sense for him to have composed this rhyming, metrical poem as a song inspired by Rolle's many similar compositions. Taking Methley as the author of this verse prayer also fits into seeing the Trinity manuscript as a kind of Methley anthology, a book collecting both his prose and poetry. In addition, the scribe Hand B appears to regard "A devout prayer" as an integral final part of *School*, because when he composed the table of contents for *School* on fol. 73^r–74^r he lists "A devout prayer on the name of Jesus" directly after the last chapter of *School* and before concluding, "Here ends the table [of contents] of the book that is called *The School of Languishing Love*." On the basis of this evidence the poem was almost certainly composed by Methley as the conclusion to *School*.

Devotion to the Holy Name of Jesus, found in the "Devout Prayer" and throughout *School*, *Bedroom*, and *Refectory*, further links Methley to Rolle as a key driver of that broader tradition. Since the eleventh century, the idea that repetition of the word *Jesus* in prayer, in an almost talismanic manner, might bring the meditant to a higher spiritual plane if not to divine union, had been growing in popularity across Europe (as well as in the

---

with Manuscript and Musical Contexts, trans. Andrew Albin (Toronto: Pontifical Institute of Mediaeval Studies, 2018), abstract.

Eastern tradition).[26] Following in the footsteps of Anselm and Bernard of Clairvaux, Rolle embraced the devotion to the Holy Name as "the most pervasive meditative practice of his teaching."[27] It can be found in, for instance, *Incendium amoris*, *Melos amoris*, *Super Canticum*, *Emendatio vitae*, and *The Commandment*. No doubt helped by Rolle's influence, by the late fourteenth century the Holy Name was a popular devotional practice throughout English society, both inside and outside the religious orders, as attested by many surviving prayers, meditations, devotional treatises, lyrics, and other texts and artifacts, as well as monograms and the Name of Jesus itself scattered through the margins of dozens of manuscripts and carved into walls and furniture. The Carthusians also had a particular interest in the Holy Name.[28]

Methley educates his readers about this devotion both didactically and demonstrably. In *School* he elaborates on the Holy Name as the "one remedy against all temptations" (chap. 14), and in *Refectory* he describes the symbolism of the letters of the name of Jesus (chap. 27). In his own prayer practice, the Holy Name functions as a way to facilitate ecstatic experience as well as to express it. "I pursued song and jubilation by invoking the name of Jesus over and over," Methley writes in chapter 22 of *Refectory*. "And look what happened! Though the bitter cold afflicted my tender body, my mind grew drunk on the sweetest melody." The

26. Denis Renevey, "Name above Names: The Devotion to the Name of Jesus from Richard Rolle to Walter Hilton's *Scale of Perfection I*," in *The Medieval Mystical Tradition, England, Ireland, and Wales: Exeter Symposium VI*, ed. Marion Glasscoe (Cambridge: D. S. Brewer, 1999), 103–21, and Bishop Kallistos [Ware], *The Power of the Name: The Jesus Prayer in Orthodox Spirituality* (Fairacres, Oxford: SLG Press, 1974).

27. Renevey, "Name Above Names," 120.

28. Brantley, *Reading in the Wilderness*, 178–95, and Denis Renevey, " 'The Name Poured Out': Margins, Illuminations, and Miniatures as Evidence for the Practice of Devotions to the Holy Name of Jesus in Late Medieval England," in *The Mystical Tradition and the Carthusians*, vol. 9, ed. James Hogg, *Analecta Cartusiana* 130 (1996): 127–47.

mystic's corporeal connection to the name of Jesus evoked here is paralleled in another moment where we get a fascinating glimpse into one of Methley's more bodily devotional techniques: "Following my usual custom, I was supposed to kiss an object, a bare post on my stall where the name of Jesus was written, while saying the words of a prayer" (*Refectory*, chap. 3). In several other passages, he records his almost uncontrollable ecstatic exclamations in the form of triplets of *Jesu*, often tripled again for a symbolically rich nine in a row (*Bedroom*, chap. 19, and *Refectory*, chap. 25, for instance). The Holy Name becomes a tool for expressing the inexpressibility of the divine as well as a way of reaching toward it.

The Holy Name tradition was intertwined with the cult of the Sacred Heart, a connection the Hand B scribe of the Trinity manuscript saw as relevant enough to Methley's works that he added a special note to the very end of Hand A's prayer concluding *School*, fol. 22^r. Here Hand B inscribes several verses originally concerning secular love: one line from Ovid's *Remedia amoris* (*Cures for Love*) and two lines from Alan of Lille's *Liber parabolarum* (*Book of Proverbs*). He appropriates them for sacred love when he inserts the well-known phrase *Jesus est amor meus* (Jesus is my love), with two linked hearts drawn around *est* and *amor*, before the apt proverb from Alan of Lille, "Whenever two hearts converge in one / It is right that they remain the same." Margery Kempe famously commissioned a ring with the motto *Jesus est amor meus* engraved on it as a symbol of her marriage to Christ (book I, chap. 31). Earlier in the fourteenth century, Henry Suso used a writing stylus to carve the holy monogram IHS onto his body over his heart. Despite the profuse bleeding, "because of his burning love he enjoyed seeing this and hardly noticed the pain," as his autobiography describes it.[29]

---

29. Henry Suso, *The Exemplar, with Two German Sermons*, trans. and ed. Frank Tobin (New York: Paulist, 1989), 70, chap. 4.

The combination of visual heart imagery with *Jesus est amor meus* also recalls another Carthusian manuscript, British Library MS Additional 37049 (ca. 1460–1470), fol. 36ᵛ, which has a detailed illustration of the holy monogram as a crucifixion scene above a large red heart through which curves a word scroll reading *est amor meus*.[30] A Carthusian monk kneels to the left of the heart at about the same scale. Below is written a composite poem concerning the Holy Name, including the first lyric in Rolle's *Ego dormio*. For that illustrator as well as for the scribe who added this note after Methley's *School*, Christ as lover was a significant aspect of the Holy Name devotion. Its erotic quality could be expressed as effectively through spoken exclamations and written repetitions, as in Methley's texts, as through visual symbols like the heart and performative devotional acts like kissing the Name carved on a wooden post.

In contrast to his engagement in Rolle's more effusive flavor of *amor sensibilis*, or "perceptible love," Methley was also firmly rooted in apophatic theology, which was in large part a Carthusian tradition of contemplative practice. Apophatic theology eschews the descriptors and sensory overload espoused by Rolle in favor of the *via negativa*: "a way of thinking and writing about God that rejects representations and seeks to stress his radical incomprehensibility and ineffability."[31] The foundational work of Christian apophaticism is *The Mystical Theology*, an originally Greek treatise attributed to the late fifth- and early sixth-century pseudo-Dionysius the Areopagite, who also wrote *The Celestial Hierarchy* and *The Divine Names*. The influence of these works was perpetu-

---

30. Brantley, *Reading in the Wilderness*, 156, 192 and plate 5.

31. Definition from "Glossary of Theological Terms," in *The Cambridge Companion to Medieval English Mysticism*, ed. Samuel Fanous and Vincent Gillespie (Cambridge: Cambridge University Press, 2011), 291. See also Andrew Louth, "Apophatic and Cataphatic Theology," in *The Cambridge Companion to Christian Mysticism*, ed. Amy Hollywood and Patricia Z. Beckman (Cambridge: Cambridge University Press, 2012), 137–46.

ated through a complex line of Latin translations, commentaries, and discussions by theologians such as John Scotus Eriugena (d. 877), Hugh of St. Victor (d. 1141), his student Richard of St. Victor (d. 1173), Thomas Gallus (or Vercellensis, d. 1246), Robert Grosseteste (d. 1253), John Sarracenus (d. 1275), Albert the Great (d. 1280), and Hugh of Balma (d. 1297).[32]

In England, the Carthusian Order showed a special interest in the pseudo-Dionysian tradition; their main sources included Sarracenus's translation, Thomas Gallus's commentaries, and Hugh of Balma's comprehensive mystical treatise *De theologia mystica* (also known by its first line, *Viae Sion lugent*, or *The Roads to Syon Mourn*), which relied on both Sarracenus and Gallus. It is possible that a late fourteenth-century English Carthusian was the translator of the Latin *Mystical Theology* into the vernacular *Deonise Hid Diuinite* (*Denis's Hidden Divinity*), though there is still some debate as to whether this person was a monk or some other kind of cleric. He also composed the Middle English masterpiece of apophatic theology *The Cloud of Unknowing*, as well as some other treatises. All these works posited that in order to reach the highest contemplative stages, and ultimately mystical union with God (*unio mystica*), one must completely "unknow" or abandon all thought and language in order to approach the divine directly. In the words of the *Cloud* author, "just as this cloud of unknowing is above you, between you and your God, in the same way you must put beneath you a cloud of forgetting, between yourself and all the creatures that have ever been made."[33]

Methley inherited this ancient tradition of the pseudo-Dionysian *via negativa*, which profoundly shaped his spirituality and his writings. The direct influence of Thomas Gallus, Hugh of Balma,

32. Jean Leclercq, "Influence and Noninfluence of Dionysius in the Western Middle Ages," in *Pseudo-Dionysius: The Complete Works*, trans. Colm Luibheid (New York: Paulist, 1987), 25–32.

33. *The Cloud of Unknowing*, trans. James Walsh (New York: Paulist, 1981), 128, chap. 5.

and the *Cloud* author can be seen in Methley's spiritual treatises, and later in his life he even translated *The Cloud of Unknowing* into Latin with extensive glosses. Like those three authors before him, Methley was in the theological camp that assigned the superior role in the unitive movement toward God to love—the loving power of the will, or affection (*affectus*)—which is not mentioned in *Mystical Theology*. This view was countered by Richard of St. Victor, Albert the Great, and, to a smaller extent, the Englishman Walter Hilton (d. 1396), who all emphasized reason or intellect (*intellectus*) as the power by which the soul is united with the divine.[34] While Hilton's *The Scale of Perfection*, book II, reveals a certain affective tendency, Hilton also warned against the extremes of Rolle's brand of sensible love and over-attachment to the Name of Jesus.[35] Chapter 17 of *School*, titled "On the form of ascent by unknowing in contemplation," positions Methley squarely in the *affectus* camp. He states right away that "no one is fit for the purest contemplation unless he first languishes for love," and, more to the point, he explains that "contemplation is above reason because, just as no one can say what God is, God cannot be seen by any effort in prayer" (chap. 17). His languishing for love, then, can also be interpreted as positing that love is the key to "the purest contemplation" and the "unknowing" that apophatic theology hails as necessary for divine union.

Throughout this chapter of *School* in particular, Methley's language closely parallels *Cloud*, suggesting that he knew the work well before he finished his translation some years later. For in-

---

34. Alastair Minnis, "Affection and Imagination in 'The Cloud of Unknowing' and Hilton's 'Scale of Perfection,'" *Traditio* 39 (1983): 323–66, at 325. See also Boyd Taylor Coolman, "The Medieval Affective Dionysian Tradition," *Modern Theology* 24 (2008): 615–32.

35. On Hilton's affective turn, see Michael Sargent, "*The Scale of Perfection* in Devotional Compilations," in *Late Medieval Devotional Compilations*, ed. Marleen Cré, Diane Denisson, and Denis Renevey (Turnhout: Brepols, 2019), 309–39. Hilton is nowhere cited in Methley's extant writings.

stance, compare Methley's direction to the reader—"You must utterly forget everything, both creation and Creator, in order to rise by unknowing"—to the short *Cloud* quotation two paragraphs above. A marginal note, probably written by Methley himself, insists on the link even more emphatically by using the precise words of the earlier work's title: "For God is found in the cloud of unknowing. Contemplation therefore is true and pure when someone is suddenly ravished above himself into that marvelous and spiritual light which is God" (chap. 17). Thomas Gallus and Hugh of Balma likewise emerge as sources not only for Methley's broader mystical approach, but also for specific turns of phrase.

In chapter 28 of *Refectory*, Methley uses the term *scintilla synderesis* or "spark of the soul," sometimes described as the "high point" of the soul.[36] In the medieval affective pseudo-Dionysian tradition, *scintilla synderesis* identifies "the highest affective part of the soul by which and through which the soul is united to God."[37] The expression could be derived from either Gallus's explanation of *The Mystical Theology* or Hugh of Balma's *Viae Sion lugent*, which itself borrowed from Gallus. As the Latin editors note, "whether Methley knew something of Hugh's book, or whether he took the expression directly from Thomas Gallus, is unclear."[38] Although he does not mention Gallus or Hugh of Balma as sources at this point, their evident influence reminds us that just behind Methley's "new material" given "by love" lies a deep well of erudition.

Another mystical source that can be discerned behind Methley's treatises is *The Mirror of Simple Souls* by the controversial French

---

36. Boyd Taylor Coolman, *Knowledge, Love, and Ecstasy in the Theology of Thomas Gallus* (Oxford: Oxford University Press, 2017), 88.

37. Steven Chase, ed. and trans., *Angelic Spirituality: Medieval Perspectives on the Ways of Angels* (New York: Paulist, 2002), 336, n. 33.

38. Clark and Hogg, *The Works*, xx. John Clark earlier states that he is "fully persuaded that Methley knew something at least of Hugh of Balma"; see *Divina caligo ignorancie: A Latin Glossed Version of* The Cloud of Unknowing, ed. John Clark, *Analecta Cartusiana* 119, no. 3 (2009): i.

mystic Marguerite Porete (d. 1310), a work that he translated into Latin around the same time as *Cloud*. Just as with *Cloud*, specific links to Porete's *Mirror* suggest that he had known the text long before he translated it. His use in chapter 34 of *Bedroom* of the metaphor of gift exchange between lovers as a way to understand humankind's relation to God could be from Porete, but perhaps her more foundational influence on Methley relates to their shared view that some kind of union with God can be a permanent state, not only a temporary one.[39] We learn much more about Methley's views on apophatic theology and advanced matters of contemplation from his glossed translations of these texts, preserved in Cambridge, Pembroke College, MS 221.[40] *Mirror* somehow appeared in England in its French form, where it was translated into Middle English by the semi-anonymous M.N., known only by those initials marking off the translator's glosses.[41] Porete's name was not attached to her text in England, so it does not appear that anyone there knew its author was a woman, much less the condemned French heretic Marguerite Porete, who was burned at the stake.

Cloud and *Mirror* are sophisticated mystical works, aiming to train advanced contemplatives in their practice and, in the case of

---

39. Methley seems to have believed that the will could be permanently united with God: "There is never a moment when I do not rejoice in the Beloved" (*Bedroom*, chap. 31). But he did not share Porete's claim to a mystical union without distinction, or "annihilation" of the soul. See Bernard McGinn, *The Flowering of Mysticism: Men and Women in the New Mysticism (1200–1350)* (New York: Crossroad, 1998), 261–65.

40. On these translations and this manuscript, as well as the modern critical tradition surrounding them, see Laura Saetveit Miles, "Richard Methley and the Translation of Vernacular Religious Writing in Latin," in *After Arundel: Religious Writing in Fifteenth-Century England*, ed. Vincent Gillespie and Kantik Ghosh (Turnhout: Brepols, 2011), 449–66.

41. On the complex history of Porete and her text, see Sean L. Field, *The Beguine, the Angel, and the Inquisitor: The Trials of Marguerite Porete and Guiard of Cressonessart* (Notre Dame, IN: University of Notre Dame Press, 2012); Robert E. Lerner, "New Light on *The Mirror of Simple Souls*," *Speculum* 85 (2010): 91–116; and Michael Sargent, "'Le Mirouer des simples âmes' and the English Mystical Tradition," *Abendländische Mystik im Mittelalter*, ed. Kurt Ruh (Stuttgart: Metzler, 1986), 443–65.

Mirror, propounding some quite unorthodox—even heretical—theology. Methley not only translated these long texts but added prologues and extensive glosses to help guide the reader to an appropriate understanding of the text, an apparatus reminiscent of *School*'s marginalia. Sara Harris has argued that Methley's interpretive glosses on Porete's *Mirror* and *Cloud* "form a commentary on the possibilities for understanding the union of the soul with God in the light of a specifically Carthusian version of discretion centered on love."[42] This program fits with the affective apophatic theology driving Methley's own corpus of spiritual treatises.

Methley intended these translations for his fellow Carthusians. A note at the end of *Cloud* specifies that he wrote it for Thurstan Watson (d. 1505), his confrère at Mount Grace. It was another Carthusian, William Darker (d. 1512/13) of Sheen, who copied the manuscript, which shows reading and annotation by a fellow Carthusian, James Grenehalgh (d. 1530), also once of Sheen, among other annotators. In producing such a translation Methley may also have hoped, as I have said elsewhere, for "transmission to mainland Europe by means of the Latin-speaking network of charterhouses or other monastic foundations which would offer an appropriate audience" at the proper elite contemplative level.[43] At the same time, however, back home in England the shift to Latin would in effect cloister such potentially problematic texts and keep them out of the reach of less advanced (lay) readers.[44] Translation into Latin also had the effect of elevating and authorizing vernacular theological texts.[45] All these aspects of translation help illuminate why Methley must have thought it both natural

42. Sara Harris, " '*In cordis tui scrinio conserua*': Richard Methley, *The Cloud of Unknowing* and Reading for Affectivity," *Marginalia* 12 (April 2011): 14–26, at 25.

43. Miles, "Richard Methley," 453.

44. Miles, "Richard Methley," 453.

45. For more on this issue see Barbara Newman, "Latin and the Vernaculars," in *The Cambridge Companion to Christian Mysticism*, ed. Amy Hollywood and Patricia Z. Beckman (Cambridge: Cambridge University Press, 2012), 225–39.

and crucial to record his own mystical experiences and contempla-tive guidance in Latin. His works were intended for a monastic audience of varying spiritual sophistication, but at least well on the way of the contemplative journey, past the earlier stages of basic prayer and meditation.

The Discernment of Spirits: *The Experience of Truth*

Methley's work *The Experience of Truth* intervenes in the long tradition of *discretio spirituum*, or discernment of spirits. *Discretio spirituum* is the ability to distinguish good or divine visitations, visions, or spiritual experiences, originating in God or angels, from bad ones originating in the devil. It was held to be a charism, a gift given by the Holy Spirit (1 Cor 12:10-11), though in the late Middle Ages, as Rosalynn Voaden says, "it had come to be under-stood that *discretio spirituum* could be acquired through learning combined with grace."[46] By the time Methley was writing, the discernment of spirits was more than a doctrine under the domain of learned clerics. Voaden argues that discernment became so widespread and shaped so much of society that it also functioned as a kind of discourse, a mode of interpreting the world through the evaluation of supernatural forces.[47]

Unfortunately, the single surviving copy of *The Experience of Truth* is missing its first half and begins in the middle of chapter 14. A marginal comment (chap. 17) indicates that chapter 6 dis-cussed evil spirits, and Michael Sargent suggests that the missing chapters dealt with "the diabolic presence, of diabolic temptations and even good thoughts diabolically inspired," as was typical for this genre.[48] Chapters 14, 15, and 16 cover issues concerning good

---

46. Rosalynn Voaden, *God's Words, Women's Voices: The Discernment of Spirits in the Writing of Late-Medieval Women Visionaries* (York, UK: York Medieval Press, 1999), 48.

47. Voaden, *God's Words, Women's Voices*, 44–46.

48. Michael Sargent, introduction to Richard Methley, "The Self-Verification of Visionary Phenomena: Richard Methley's '*Experimentum Veritatis*,'" ed. Michael

and bad angels, a recurring topic in Methley's autobiographical works. Then he moves on to a list of questions for discerning the veracity of visions or aural locutions in chapter 17. Chapters 18, 19, and 20 discuss how to test and when to believe "evangelists and prophets of modern times," without specifying who they might be. The next four chapters seem tailored to an audience of Methley's fellow monks, as they were not typical topics for *discretio spirituum* treatises. Evidently Carthusians as "holy men" were called on to help theologians reach an agreement on scholastic or spiritual matters, as chapter 21 implies. Chapter 22 prepares such a "man of God" for the eventuality that others might not believe him and might question the veracity of his mystical experiences or divine revelations. Methley dismisses the skeptics and errs on the side of the visionary, prioritizing the power of the Holy Spirit to teach discernment over that of humans.

Chapter 23 shifts gears to explain that it is generally not a problem for bishops or pastors to leave the active life in the world and take up a contemplative life, while chapter 24 encourages the solitary contemplative to resist any desire on his own part to abandon the hermitage for a public life of preaching. A more personal, reflective turn drives the next chapter, where Methley describes his status as a respected, sought-after authority in mystical matters. Others frequently ask him, he says, "how to attain divine love," and he feels divinely obligated to disseminate his experiences and knowledge. To follow through on this promise, in chapter 26 he briefly lists seven necessary beliefs or ways of living to achieve that divine love. The concluding chapter directs its readers to ask God for help in understanding matters presented in the treatise, and to maintain virtuous chastity and, if possible, virginity.

As this summary suggests, Methley bases much of this text on his own visionary and mystical experience. He declares this himself when he explains the choice of title: "It is *The Experience of*

Truth that I write, for I have learned these things by feeling them directly in the spirit" (chap. 24). While earlier authorities such as Alfonso of Jaén (d. 1389) and Jean Gerson (d. 1429) recommend that a clerical expert in discernment "should himself have had transcendental experiences," it is not evident that any of them actually attained the highest levels of advanced contemplation, much less rapture, as Methley claims for himself.[49] Gerson, for example, emphasizes his lack of qualification to write about mystical experiences, while Walter Hilton allows that a devout, perfect soul may experience bodily feelings of divine ecstasy, but adds the caveat, "I know not whether there be any such man living on earth."[50] Thus Methley's treatise may well be one of the sole surviving *discretio spirituum* treatises written by a practicing male mystic. (Catherine of Siena also writes about discernment.[51]) To support his advice about discernment he frequently cites personal visitations by angels and devils, especially in chapter 15, where he writes that he will "explain as best I can, with God's guidance, what I have learned from experience about these good and bad angels." These anecdotes echo episodes documented in *School*, such as chapter 31, where the devil sits on his right foot, and *Refectory*, chapters 11, 31, 32, and 38.

Methley demonstrates a general (though perhaps spotty) familiarity with the tradition of *discretio spirituum*, as shaped by the classic works of Cassian (d. 435), Augustine (d. 430), Hugh of St. Victor (d. 1141), Thomas Aquinas (d. 1274), Alfonso of Jaén, and Jean Gerson. Two late fourteenth-century Middle English works dealing with discernment seem likely to have been known by

---

49. Voaden, *God's Words, Women's Voices*, 58.

50. Catherine Brown, *Pastor and Laity in the Theology of Jean Gerson* (Cambridge: Cambridge University Press, 1987), 205; Walter Hilton, *The Scale of Perfection*, ed. Thomas H. Bestul (Kalamazoo, MI: Medieval Institute Publications, 2000), 42, lines 262–63 (book I, chap. 11), my modernization.

51. See Jennifer N. Brown, *Fruit of the Orchard: Reading Catherine of Siena in Late Medieval and Early Modern England* (Toronto: University of Toronto Press, 2019), 101–6.

Methley, though he does not cite them explicitly: the *Cloud* author's text *A Tretis of Discrecyon of Spirites* and Hilton's *The Scale of Perfection*. In contrast to his reliance on Rolle in his spiritual treatises, Methley does not mention, cite, or allude even indirectly to any specific authorities on discernment beyond himself. A rare exception is his reference to Augustine's well-known hierarchy of corporeal, spiritual, and intellectual visions, from *The Literal Meaning of Genesis*. This classification system shaped all medieval treatises that concerned visions, and it is that reception that Methley refers to in chapter 17: "If these types of vision are properly interpreted in their place, I believe the books of contemplatives always say that ecstasy and spiritual vision assume the forms of objects in the spirit."[52] Without naming Augustine specifically, his reference to the textual authority of "books of contemplatives" demonstrates the reliability of this formal categorization of visions, which undergirds his autobiographical treatises as well. But for the rest of the treatise, his own experience suffices as authority enough.

Methley sometimes departs substantially from mainstream discernment practices. Gerson, the *Cloud* author, and Hilton, for instance, all stipulate meticulous adherence to a thorough *discretio* process and adopt a posture of suspicion toward such experiences rather than embracing or encouraging them. Hilton's *Scale* warns against perceptible signs such as the song, sweetness, and heat of Rollean spirituality, or the appearance of angels: "be then wary at that time and soon after."[53] He says that the bodily feeling of heavenly joy, when accompanied by the desire to leave off active prayer and thinking, is especially "suspect and of the enemy." In contrast to this tendency toward caution, Methley often takes a position of radical affirmation.

Perhaps his unique method of drawing on his own mystical experience lies behind this. For instance, in chapter 17 he identifies

---

52. See Augustine, *The Literal Meaning of Genesis: Books 7–12*, trans. J. H. Taylor (New York: Paulist, 1982), 186.

53. Hilton, *The Scale*, 41, lines 231–32 (book I, chap. 11).

five steps in the discernment of revelations, the first three of which roughly match Gerson's in his *De probatione spirituum* (*On the Testing of Spirits*). In a clear departure from Gerson, however, Methley adds an emphasis on the perceptible love or *amor sensibilis* that shapes his own spirituality: "Before I proceed any further, let me say that if such a person is constant and truthful, and has the perceptible divine love that I discussed above, I simply affirm that he or she should be believed." To stop there and "simply affirm" the visions' validity without further probing is quite bold. He makes such affirmations several times in this chapter and elsewhere. In contrast, for instance, the French theologian Pierre d'Ailly (d. 1420) warns strongly against trusting people who believed in their own truth without external confirmation, as they "often did not know themselves for the seducers and hypocrites that they were, instead regarding themselves as saints who had truly conquered sin."[54] Methley pushes back against such doubt in favor of accepting God's presence and supporting the faithful individual, a sentiment summed up in a memorable line from chapter 18: "We should always choose what is better, safer, and kinder."

The treatise's tone conveys the confidence of an established spiritual director, and the treatise itself seems to have been written at the request of others seeking Methley's expertise as rooted in his experience. It was crucial to the process of *discretio spirituum* that the spiritual director be a priest or confessor who could verify and support the visionary's vocation, and it constituted "the first line of defense in the Church's battle against demonic infiltration."[55] Yet just as Methley declines to defer to others' authority in the textual discernment tradition, he consistently underplays the role of the spiritual director as the foremost authority in discernment. Rather, he says that it is the contemplative who should trust him-

---

54. Dyan Elliott, *Proving Woman: Female Spirituality and Inquisitional Culture in the Later Middle Ages* (Princeton: Princeton University Press, 2004), 261.

55. Voaden, *God's Words, Women's Voices*, 57.

self or herself, relying on the Holy Spirit for direction. "The Holy Spirit will teach you if there is no human being you can trust in spiritual matters," he counsels in chapter 22, a sentiment that would surely strike Gerson and Hilton as leading the visionary dangerously astray from the authority of the church.

Yet for Methley, the bigger risk is to ignore "God's modern prophets," either because one's own errors are being exposed by the prophecy, or simply because others have falsely prophesied in the past. He does warn the visionary reader to "discern well," and "so as the Holy Spirit teaches you, be silent, or else entrust the revelation to your superiors for their judgment." But this is one of very few places where he advises deferring to a spiritual director or confessor as a higher authority. And indeed, in the very next sentence, he reverts to God as the ultimate authority in whom trust should be placed: "There is no doubt that the One who created you can teach you rightly" (chap. 22). The implication is that humans, compromised by excessive caution or even sin, present the worse danger of undervaluing legitimate divine presence or teaching wrongly.

This unusual confidence in mystical and prophetic claims raises the interesting question of the intended audience of *Experience* and the relationship of Methley's advice to the main objects of discernment in the later Middle Ages: female visionaries. In the last chapter, he addresses his "sweetest and most blessed fathers, brothers, and sisters," suggesting, for the first and only time in his works, an audience of both men and women. This mention of sisters could mean that he intended the text either for enclosed women in other orders in England, or for Carthusian sisters on the Continent. But earlier in the treatise, as we have seen, he still seems to envision a primarily enclosed male audience for *Experience*, as when he refers to the reader as a "man of God" and addresses problems specific to Carthusians and male hermits. Whether men and/or women, however, his audience seems to occupy a quite advanced or initiated position, at or near the level of spiritual directors themselves.

This enclosed audience could stand in contrast to the laywomen that other authors who wrote treatises on discernment were so concerned about—vocal, unenclosed visionaries like Birgitta of Sweden, whom Gerson saw as a dangerous precedent liable to lead souls astray, and Margery Kempe. As *To Hugh Hermit* shows, Methley had pastoral duties outside the charterhouse to some extent, at least as spiritual director to a local hermit. But there is no evidence that such direction might have extended further to laymen or women experiencing visions. Such a readership of professional contemplatives might explain Methley's rather unorthodox encouragement of mystical visionary experiences, or it may be his own experience of truth, as a mystic immersed in the perceptible love of God, that prevents him from adopting the skepticism of Gerson or Hilton. Unlike those clerics, he firmly believed that "God's modern prophets" existed in his day, perhaps because he saw himself as one of them—and he probably recognized fellow "modern prophets" in some of his own Carthusian brothers, a point to which I will return.

Carthusian Pastoral Care: *To Hugh Hermit*

The letter Methley wrote to a local hermit named Hugh offers an example of the pastoral care, textual and otherwise, that Carthusian monks offered to people who lived both within and outside their own charterhouse walls. The order had long been responsible for offering sacraments and spiritual direction to the lay brethren and servants who helped the monks maintain their eremitic lifestyle, and these duties began extending (sometimes problematically) to the local community and lay benefactors as the Carthusians expanded and increasingly relied on outside funding.[56] As was fitting with their strong book culture, the Carthusians also

---

56. Vincent Gillespie, *"Cura Pastoralis in Deserto,"* in *Looking in Holy Books: Essays on Late Medieval Religious Writing in England* (Turnhout: Brepols, 2011), 21–48. On Methley's appearance in contemporary wills of local lay people, see Clark, *Divina caligo ignorancie*, ix.

provided spiritual support to others through the composition and copying of texts, or "preaching with the hands." A few previous precedents of vernacular devotional outreach survive from England.[57] Almost a hundred years earlier, Nicholas Love (d. 1424), monk and prior of Mount Grace, had transformed the famous pseudo-Bonaventuran *Meditationes vitae Christi* into a new vernacular version, *Mirror of the Blessed Life of Jesus Christ*. This long gospel meditation gained ecclesiastical approval and became quite popular, circulating widely among both lay and monastic readers. Some time later an anonymous monk from Sheen Charterhouse created a similar devotional text, *Mirror to Devout People* (*Speculum devotorum*), composed for the Birgittine sisters of neighboring Syon Abbey. It too achieved a broader lay and monastic circulation. Either one would have been an appropriate "holy English book" for Hugh to read.

To Hugh Hermit: An Epistle on Solitary Life Nowadays is a bit different from these other works in that it is directed to an individual reader—a hermit named Hugh (though of course Methley might have imagined a wider readership as well). Both the Carthusian Order in general and Methley in particular had special relationships to non-monastic hermits living a strictly eremitical life parallel to their own. For instance, when King Henry V founded Sheen in 1414, he obliged the monks to take care of a nearby hermit, so perhaps this was an established tradition at the other charterhouses as well.[58] Mount Grace was also in a county quite populated with hermits, at least relatively speaking: there are records of a hundred recluses in Yorkshire, more than any other county.[59] Perhaps some of these were inspired by the legacy of their local celebrity hermit, Richard Rolle. There were certainly

---

57. For a full account of English vernacular theology from the Anglo-Saxon period onward, see Nicholas Watson, *Balaam's Ass: Vernacular Theology Before the English Reformation*, 2 vols. (Philadelphia: University of Pennsylvania Press, forthcoming).

58. Brantley, *Reading in the Wilderness*, 45.

59. Rotha Mary Clay, *The Hermits and Anchorites of England* (London: Methuen, 1913), Appendix C, 254–61.

many more hermits, recluses, and anchorites historically than are noted in surviving documents, including the recipient of this letter. We do not seem to have any record of a recluse named Hugh in this period and region connected to a chapel of Our Lady, as Methley specifies in chapter 3.

Be that as it may, by the late fifteenth and early sixteenth centuries, it is not surprising that Methley was acting as a spiritual director for a local hermit who had chosen a reclusive lifestyle but without a vow binding him to a religious order.[60] Methley perhaps felt a kinship with Hugh, as he also saw himself as a kind of hermit, sometimes referring to himself and other Carthusians as *solitarii*. He was also inspired to join such a solitary order because of an interaction with another recluse, an old anchoress, as discussed above. The letter points to how solitaries might aspire to solitude and at the same time be enmeshed in a vibrant virtual network of holy men and women connected by mentorship, reputation, personal letters, commissioned compositions, and manuscript transmission.[61] While Methley warned Hugh against contact with lay people seeking his counsel at the risk of drawing him away from his cell ("you are sent to visit nobles in the country, whom you dare not displease" [chap. 9]), there was no conflict in one solitary's reaching out to another, seeking support for a life of prayer and contemplation.

In this epistle, as in his spiritual treatises, Methley chooses a scriptural verse around which to weave his prose: Psalm 142:9-10, "Lord, deliver me from my enemies; to thee I have fled; teach me to do thy will, for thou art my God." Again this refrain offers

60. Brantley raises the possibility that he could have been a Carthusian, despite the letter's comments suggesting that he had traveled outside his enclosure: *Reading in the Wilderness*, 343, n. 63.

61. For a related view on the anchoress Julian of Norwich, "isolated" in her cell even as she was centered physically and spiritually in a bustling city, see Laura Saetveit Miles, "Space and Enclosure in Julian of Norwich's *A Revelation of Love*," in *A Companion to Julian of Norwich*, ed. Liz Herbert McAvoy (Cambridge: Boydell and Brewer, 2008), 154–65.

content for Methley to discuss as well as functioning as a prayer for Hugh to perform. Over twelve short chapters Methley manages to cover a solid base of traditional advice for "solitary living." He first introduces three "enemies"—the world, one's flesh, and the devil—and then details the three traditional monastic virtues that can overcome them: poverty, chastity, and obedience, respectively. Next come the specifics of how to behave properly as a solitary, with three things to "guard well" or keep: one's sight, the cell itself, and silence. The final two chapters move on to present what Hugh should actually do with his time, specifically five activities: 1) prayer, 2) meditation, 3) reading of "holy English books," 4) contemplation, and 5) "good deeds with your hands" (chap. 11). According to the final chapter, his day should begin and end with "long prayers or other spiritual exercises like meditation," and the time between such exercises should be filled with "many prayers or spiritual exercises, but briefly and often" interspersed with "work," presumably the "good deeds" just mentioned.

Methley's directions echo traditional advice to solitaries found in classic Carthusian writings and other influential texts of contemplative guidance. The Carthusian monk Guigo II (d. 1188), ninth prior of the Grande Chartreuse, is linked to a popular text called *Scala claustralium* (*The Ladder for Monks*), which identifies four rungs of spiritual work on a ladder leading up to mystical communion with God: reading, meditation, prayer, and contemplation (*lectio, meditatio, oratio, contemplatio*). Methley was doubtless familiar with this foundational work of prayer guidance. Even Hugh himself might have known the *Scala* in its vernacular translation and expansion, *A Ladder of Foure Ronges by the which Men Mowe Wele Clyme to Heven* (*A Ladder of Four Rungs by Which Men May Well Climb to Heaven*), targeting religious and lay readers, and another ideal "holy English book" for him to read.[62] A later insular Carthusian author, Adam of Dryburgh

---

62. One copy of *Foure Ronges*, Cambridge University Library Ff.6.33, was copied by the Carthusian monk William Darker, also the scribe of Methley's Latin translations of *Cloud* and *Mirror*.

(d. ca. 1212), monk at Witham Charterhouse in Somerset and former Premonstratensian, included good deeds alongside reading, prayer, and meditation in his treatise *De quadripartito exercitio cellae* (*The Fourfold Exercise of the Cell*). These two contributions joined an eleventh- and twelfth-century surge of works of spiritual guidance for those seeking a contemplative life, both men and women, in the genres of letters of spiritual counsel and anchoritic guides. The Cistercian Aelred of Rievaulx, for instance, composed *De institutione inclusarum*, or *The Formation of Recluses* (later translated into Middle English twice), while an anonymous cleric wrote the vernacular *Ancrene Wisse* between about 1225 and 1240. Both provide an enclosed female audience with detailed instructions for the outer and inner life of the anchoress, doing the same duty as Methley's letter but in much greater depth.

One difference, notably, is that these texts for women do not typically enjoin their readers to reach for the heights of mystical union with the divine, as Methley does when he urges Hugh toward contemplation, which, he says, in its purest form, "you may attain by means of grace and great devotion, that is, to forget all manner of things except God, and for great love of him to be rapt into contemplation" (chap. 11). This one passing mention of the forgetting that constitutes true ecstasy suggests that Methley thought it appropriate for Hugh at least to be aware of a more advanced apophatic approach, as taught by *Cloud* and expounded in his own spiritual works. But tellingly, he did not see fit to give him any tools to aid him further on the *via negativa*. That textual tradition and most of Rolle's works would have been unavailable to Hugh, who could not read Latin, as Methley painstakingly translated every single Latin word in his letter to him. Should we imagine Hugh as the kind of reader that Methley might have wished to shut out of *Cloud* and *Mirror* by translating them from the vernacular into Latin? The *lingua franca* of the *litterati* had the power to exclude untrained readers just down the road, even as it opened up audiences all across Europe.

Methley's Audience and Subsequent Influence

Who read Methley's works? How influential was he? For the spiritual treatises of *School*, *Bedroom*, and *Refectory*, Methley consistently addresses his "brothers" as the reading audience, and refers to his vocation as a monk or sometimes hermit (*solitarius*) in a way that suggests that his readers shared the same contemplative life (even if they were not all at his level of spiritual sophistication or state of grace). The manuscript evidence confirms this textual evidence. The Trinity manuscript, discussed above, shows how Carthusians copied the spiritual treatises and annotated them for reading within the charterhouse, whether that was Mount Grace or elsewhere. Methley's works were studied and respected by at least this coterie of monastic readers of the late fifteenth to mid-sixteenth centuries. *Experience* and *To Hugh Hermit*, on the other hand, were intended for slightly different audiences. As was mentioned above, *Experience* addresses Methley's fellow monks (*patres et fratres*) but also "sisters" (*sorores*), suggesting that he intended the work to travel outside the network of English charterhouses and to be read by female religious of some kind, either in England or abroad (Carthusian nuns were only found on the Continent). *To Hugh Hermit*, of course, was written for a fellow contemplative who did not share the same profession, strict enclosure, or education as Methley, but who fell under the pastoral care of the Carthusians—though we have no way to know if Hugh or other readers received the text and what they thought of it.

We do have one exceptional proof of Methley's broader influence in English religious culture. Perhaps the best-known reference to Methley can be found in the margins of the *Book* of Margery Kempe: London, British Library, Additional MS 61823. This is the single surviving copy of a fascinating text about the spiritual experiences, visions, pilgrimages, and saintly life of the English laywoman Margery Kempe. In the late Middle Ages Mount Grace Charterhouse came to own the manuscript, and one of its monks commented extensively in its margins in a distinctive

red ink. He is now known to scholars as the "red ink annotator."
Throughout the manuscript this annotator repeatedly references
Richard Methley, his fellow Carthusian John Norton (d.
1522), and Richard Rolle in order to "endorse or authorize Margery's
affective mystical experiences" for a monastic audience, and possibly even for "the devotional use of an audience of lay women,"
as Kelly Parsons argues, somewhat controversially.[63] At least three
marginal comments mention Methley as a positive comparison
for the excessive weeping and affective devotion expressed by
Kempe—or perhaps vice versa; Kempe's precedent helped to
authorize Methley's similar spirituality many decades later. For
instance, at the end of chapter 13 of the *Book*, this annotator
writes, "R. Medley v[icar] was wont so to say" in red in the margin
beside a passage describing Kempe's daily contemplative and
mystical experiences: "with many sweet tears of high devotion so
abundantly and continually that it was a marvel that her eyes
endured, or that her heart could last without being consumed with
the ardor of love which was kindled with the holy converse of our
Lord."[64] Here the reference to the fire of love evokes Rolle as a
common inspiration behind Methley and Kempe, and the description of Kempe's holy crying recalls how in *Refectory* Methley
writes of "groaning and weeping" (chap. 7).

---

63. Book I, chap. 13 (p. 97), chap. 28 (p. 164), and chap. 73 (p. 323), in *The Book of Margery Kempe*, ed. Barry Windeatt (Cambridge: D. S. Brewer, 2004); and Kelly Parsons, "The Red Ink Annotator of *The Book of Margery Kempe* and His Lay Audience," in *The Medieval Professional Reader at Work: Evidence from Chaucer, Langland, Kempe, and Gower*, ed. Kathryn Kerby-Fulton, Maidie Hilmo, and Linda Olson (Victoria, BC: English Literary Studies, 2001), 143–216, at 144 (see 164–216 for a full list of the red-ink annotations, corrections, and rubrications). On the view that Carthusians did not necessarily promulgate "such materials to the laity," see Vincent Gillespie, "1412–1534: Culture and History," in *The Cambridge Companion to Medieval English Mysticism*, ed. Gillespie and Samuel Fanous (Cambridge: Cambridge University Press, 2011), 170.

64. Margery Kempe, *The Book of Margery Kempe*, trans. Barry Windeatt (London: Penguin, 1985), 64.

Referring to what Methley "was wont so to say" in the past tense suggests that the annotations were written after his death, between about 1528 and 1538. This wording also implies that the annotator knew Methley personally and had even heard him speak frequently of his experiences, and wanted to remind his readers of Methley's memory and his extraordinary spirituality. Later, in chapter 28, the marginal annotation "so fa [father] RM & f [father] Norton of Wakenes & of the passion" is written by the following description of Kempe's boisterous tears: "The crying was so loud and so amazing that it astounded people, unless they had heard it before, or else knew the reason for the cryings. And she had them so often that they made her very weak in her bodily strength, and specially if she heard our Lord's Passion."[65] This marginal comment, like some of the others by this annotator, emphasizes that Kempe, Methley, and Norton shared a bodily aspect of their performative spirituality. Seeing the goal of the red ink annotations as "research into the true nature of visionary experience"—typically Carthusian, I would add—helps to explain this monk's sincere interest, rather than skepticism, concerning more extreme corporeal expressions of divine encounters.[66]

Examining the red ink annotator's comparison of Kempe and Methley reveals many seeming contradictions that were not necessarily perceived as contradictions by this kind of reader. As a Carthusian monk far removed in time and space from Kempe's busy, social lay life, the red ink annotator nonetheless took the *Book* extremely seriously. He deeply approved of Kempe's literary-devotional project and took many opportunities to affirm her style of affective, bodily spirituality, and to align it with the experiences of his fellow monks. Karma Lochrie suggests that we should take

---

65. *Book*, trans. Windeatt, 104.

66. Kathryn Kerby-Fulton, "Professional Readers at Work: Annotators, Editors, and Correctors in Middle English Literary Texts," in *Opening Up Middle English Manuscripts: Literary and Visual Approaches*, ed. Kathryn Kerby-Fulton, Maidie Hilmo, and Linda Olson (Ithaca, NY: Cornell University Press, 2012), 238.

careful heed of the evidence that Methley saw no incompatibility between "monastic vocation and 'excessive sensory devotion,' or between that devotion and 'pure contemplation.'"[67] Likewise the red ink annotator, I suggest, could have seen Methley and Kempe's shared experience of *amor sensibilis*—the love of God perceptible by the heart, senses, and body—as helping to override differences in gender or vocation. Kempe's *Book* was intended to be a universal story of a holy life offered as a comfort and inspiration to fellow and future Christians.[68] In contrast, modern readers sometimes risk overemphasizing the historical and autobiographical aspects (important though they are) at the expense of taking the *Book* seriously as a spiritual treatise. Reading Methley's spiritual diaries as another kind of early autobiography provides a crucial comparative datapoint for understanding Margery Kempe and her book that would reward further analysis.

As these examples attest, the red ink annotator expected his intended readers to have known of Methley, either by reputation or by reading his texts, and to come to a better understanding of both Methley's and Kempe's experiences by seeing their similarities. This audience undoubtedly included Carthusian monks, but also possibly extended outside the monastery to lay readers, both men and women, for whom the Carthusians provided pastoral care.[69] Would Methley and his mysticism have been known by laity connected to Mount Grace? It seems possible, though the red-ink annotations might be our only evidence. How far outside north Yorkshire his reputation traveled is impossible to tell; certainly not as widely as that of his predecessor Richard Rolle, though Rolle's popularity does set a precedent for Methley's broader reception. Regardless, these annotations suggest that

---

67. Karma Lochrie, *Margery Kempe and Translations of the Flesh* (Philadelphia: University of Pennsylvania Press, 1994), 217.

68. Lochrie, *Margery Kempe*, 226. On this theme see Rebecca Krug, *Margery Kempe and the Lonely Reader* (Ithaca, NY: Cornell University Press, 2017).

69. Parsons, "The Red Ink Annotator."

Methley and Kempe were highly regarded for both their perfect contemplation *and* their intense outbursts, among other things, by both monks *and* aristocratic women and men.

In these affirmative annotations we can see a fulfillment of Methley's strong desire to have others read and learn from his experiences—an outward-facing, pastoral desire shared by Kempe and Rolle. Katherine Zieman identifies Methley, Kempe, and Rolle as "public contemplatives" who produce "a category of contemplative writings that are inseparable from the identities of their authors." Such writings "must construct and represent the self as a series of experiences as much as they represent the divine to their audiences." [70] Methley was not going to bury his talent, or spiritual gift (Matt 25:14-30), behind his eremitic vocation. While he was restricted from traveling the country or the world as Kempe did, his reputation seems to have extended beyond the charterhouse walls, and the surviving single witnesses to his writings could be but small traces of his wider renown.

Importantly, Methley seems to be part of an increasingly active movement of Carthusian visionary spirituality, concentrated at Mount Grace, from the last quarter of the fifteenth century up to the Reformation. John Norton, whom the red ink annotator mentioned alongside Methley as sharing a similar, highly performative religiosity, professed as a Carthusian in 1482 and was sixth prior at Mount Grace until his death in 1522. [71] His three surviving works in Lincoln Cathedral, MS 57, *Musica monachorum* (*Music of Monks*), *Thesaurus cordium amantium* (*Treasury of Loving Hearts*), and *Devota lamentatio* (*Devout Lamentation*), discuss his own visions and Christic locutions as well as monastic life more generally, though at not quite the same level of sophistication as those of his confrère Methley. Norton had a vision of the Virgin Mary in the habit of a Carthusian nun and supposedly

70. Zieman, "Monasticism and the Public Contemplative," 700–701.

71. John Norton, *The Works of John Norton*, ed. John Clark and James Hogg, *Analecta Cartusiana* 64, no. 3 (2016): xi–xii.

foretold the proliferation of Carthusian houses;[72] perhaps he hoped to see the Order establish a nunnery in England. His works were only recently edited and remain untranslated.

Twelve years after Norton's death, and six or seven after Methley's, another Mount Grace monk was reported as having visions in a letter written from a Carthusian to Henry VIII, dated August 6, 1534: "At Mountgrace there is a brother who has revelations, though I cannot tell what they be, but he bears a great name in our religion. . . . His name is Fletcher."[73] The same Robert Fletcher was also the addressee of introductory epistles written by William Melton, chancellor of York Cathedral, discussing Norton's works and included in the Lincoln MS. These clues begin to paint a picture of a monastic community that not only tolerated but encouraged mystical experiences, and cultivated reverence for those that passed the scrutiny of the *discretio spirituum* process detailed in Methley's treatise. If Fletcher "bears a great name in our religion," we can imagine his reputation building on the even stronger reputations of his visionary predecessors at Mount Grace, Methley and Norton, who might have been better known because of their authorship. (Nothing ascribed to Fletcher survives.[74]) Methley overlapped with Norton for all forty years of the latter's profession. According to Tekla Bude's groundbreaking work on

---

72. Norton, *Works*, xv.

73. "Henry VIII: August 1534, 6–10," in *Letters and Papers, Foreign and Domestic, Henry VIII, Volume 7, 1534*, ed. James Gairdner (London: Her Majesty's Stationery Office, 1883), 407–12. *British History Online*, accessed November 6, 2019, http://www.british-history.ac.uk/letters-papers-hen8/vol7/pp407-412. Some bias in the letter writer must be taken into account, as the letter also states, "I trust his revelations may prove better than those of the Maid of Kent" (referring to Elizabeth Barton, a controversial visionary executed in 1534), and then continues, "One of the monks at Mountgrace was buried in a dunghill, why I cannot tell. The prior and his convent will defend it as much as they can, but I think it not lawful to bury their brother in a dunghill for breaking of a poor ceremony."

74. He is, however, the protagonist of Lucy Beckett's novel about the Dissolution at Mount Grace: *The Time Before You Die: A Novel of the Reformation* (San Francisco: Ignatius Press, 1999).

these two figures and their remarkable productions, we must consider "the role of Carthusian *fraternitas* in recasting Rollean mysticism as something collaborative and textual rather than singular and sonic."[75] Methley and Norton could have been eyewitnesses for each other's raptures when they occurred in communal settings outside the cell. They could have been key partners in each other's discernment process, and they probably read each other's texts or even drafts. Their confrères Thurstan Watson, William Darker, and James Grenehalgh (among many other anonymous brothers) read, copied, and commented on their works, disseminating them throughout the order and perhaps beyond. For the decades of Methley's profession and up to the eve of the Dissolution, Mount Grace appears to have nurtured a thriving culture of mystical practice unparalleled in late-medieval England, and nowhere better attested than in the texts of this volume.

---

75. Tekla Bude, from her monograph in progress, *Sonic Bodies: Text, Music, and Silence in Late Medieval England.*

Selected Bibliography

Texts

Adam of Witham [aka Adam of Dryburgh]. *De quadripartito exercitio cellae. A Critical Edition.* 2 vols. Edited by John Clark and James Hogg. *Analecta Cartusiana* 256, nos. 1–2 (2015).

Clark, John P. H., ed. *The Latin Versions of* The Cloud of Unknowing. 2 vols. *Analecta Cartusiana* 119 (1989).

Guigo II. *The Ladder of Monks: A Letter on the Contemplative Life* and *Twelve Meditations.* Translated by Edmund Colledge and James Walsh. CS 48. Kalamazoo, MI: Cistercian Publications, 1981.

Hilton, Walter. *The Scale of Perfection.* Translated by John P. H. Clark and Rosemary Dorward. New York: Paulist, 1991.

Hodgson, Phyllis, ed. *The Cloud of Unknowing and Related Treatises on Contemplative Prayer. Analecta Cartusiana* 3 (1982).

———. *Deonise Hid Divinite and Other Treatises on Contemplative Prayer.* EETS o.s. 231. London: Oxford University Press, 1955.

Hugh of Balma and Guigo de Ponte. *Carthusian Spirituality: The Writings of Hugh of Balma and Guigo de Ponte.* Translated by Dennis Martin. New York: Paulist, 1997.

Kempe, Margery. *The Book of Margery Kempe.* Translated by Barry Windeatt. London: Penguin, 1985.

Methley, Richard. *Divina caligo ignorancie: A Latin Glossed Version of* The Cloud of Unknowing. Edited by John Clark. *Analecta Cartusiana* 119, no. 3 (2009).

———. "The *Dormitorium dilecti Dilecti* of Richard Methley of Mount Grace Charterhouse, transcribed from the Trinity College Cambridge MS O.2.56." Edited by James Hogg. *Analecta Cartusiana* 55, no. 5 (1982): 79–103.

————. "A Mystical Diary: The *Refectorium salutis* of Richard Methley of Mount Grace Charterhouse." Edited by James Hogg. *Analecta Cartusiana* 55, no. 1 (1981): 208–38.

————. "Richard Methley: To Hew Heremyte, A Pystyl of Solytary Lyfe Nowadayes." Edited by James Hogg. *Analecta Cartusiana* 31 (1977): 91–119.

————. "The *Scola amoris languidi* of Richard Methley of Mount Grace Charterhouse, transcribed from the Trinity College Cambridge MS O.2.56." Edited by James Hogg. *Analecta Cartusiana* 55, no. 2 (1981): 138–65.

————. "The Self-Verification of Visionary Phenomena: Richard Methley's '*Experimentum Veritatis*.' " Edited by Michael Sargent. *Analecta Cartusiana* 55, no. 2 (1981): 121–37.

————. *Speculum animarum simplicium: A Glossed Latin Version of* The Mirror of Simple Souls. Edited by John Clark. *Analecta Cartusiana* 266, no. 1–2 (2010).

————. *The Works of Richard Methley*. Edited by John Clark and James Hogg. *Analecta Cartusiana* 64, no. 1 (2017).

Norton, John. *The Works of John Norton*. Edited by John Clark and James Hogg. *Analecta Cartusiana* 64, no. 3 (2016).

Porete, Marguerite. *The Mirror of Simple Souls*. Translated by Ellen L. Babinsky. New York: Paulist, 1993.

Rolle, Richard. *Emendatio Vitae; Orationes ad Honorem Nominis Ihesu*. Edited by Nicholas Watson. Toronto: Pontifical Institute of Mediaeval Studies, 1995.

————. *The English Works*. Translated by Rosamund S. Allen. New York: Paulist, 1988.

————. *Richard Rolle: Prose and Verse*. Edited by S. J. Ogilvie-Thomson. EETS o.s. 293. Oxford: Oxford University Press, 1988.

————. *Richard Rolle's* Melody of Love*: A Study and Translation with Manuscript and Musical Contexts*. Translated by Andrew Albin. Toronto: Pontifical Institute of Mediaeval Studies, 2018.

Walsh, James, trans. *The Cloud of Unknowing*. New York: Paulist, 1981.

Studies

Anderson, Wendy Love. *The Discernment of Spirits: Assessing Visions and Visionaries in the Late Middle Ages*. Tübingen: Mohr Siebeck, 2011.

Brantley, Jessica. *Reading in the Wilderness: Private Devotion and Public Performance in Late Medieval England.* Chicago: University of Chicago Press, 2007.

Clay, Rotha Mary. *The Hermits and Anchorites of England.* London: Methuen, 1913.

Coolman, Boyd Taylor. "The Medieval Affective Dionysian Tradition." *Modern Theology* 24 (2008): 615–32.

Coppack, Glyn, and Mick Aston. *Christ's Poor Men: The Carthusians in England.* Stroud, Gloucs. Tempus, 2002.

Cré, Marleen. *Vernacular Mysticism in the Charterhouse: A Study of London, British Library, MS Additional 37790.* Turnhout: Brepols, 2006.

Doyle, A. I. "Carthusian Participation in the Movement of Works of Richard Rolle between England and Other Parts of Europe in the 14th and 15th Centuries." *Analecta Cartusiana* 55, no. 2 (1981): 109–20.

———. "The Carthusians." In *Syon Abbey, with the Libraries of the Carthusians*, edited by Vincent Gillespie and A. I. Doyle. London: British Library, 2001. 601–52.

Gillespie, Vincent. "*Cura Pastoralis in Deserto.*" In *Looking in Holy Books: Essays on Late Medieval Religious Writing in England.* Turnhout: Brepols, 2011. 21–48.

———. "1412–1534: Culture and History." In *The Cambridge Companion to Medieval English Mysticism*, edited by Vincent Gillespie and Samuel Fanous. Cambridge: Cambridge University Press, 2011. 163–94.

Harris, Sara. " '*In cordis tui scrinio conserua*': Richard Methley, *The Cloud of Unknowing* and Reading for Affectivity." *Marginalia* 12 (April 2011): 14–26.

Hogg, James. "Mount Grace Charterhouse and Late Medieval English Spirituality." *Analecta Cartusiana* 82, no. 3 (1978): 1–43.

Kerby-Fulton, Kathryn. "Professional Readers at Work: Annotators, Editors, and Correctors in Middle English Literary Texts." In *Opening Up Middle English Manuscripts: Literary and Visual Approaches*, edited by Kathryn Kerby-Fulton, Maidie Hilmo, and Linda Olson. Ithaca, NY: Cornell University Press, 2012. 207–44.

Knowles, David. "Developments within the Orders, Part II: The Carthusians." *The Religious Orders in England.* 3 vols. Cambridge: Cambridge University Press, 1955. 2:129–38.

Large, J. A. "The Libraries of the Carthusian Order in Medieval England." *Library History* 3 (1975): 191–203.

Lockhart, Robin Bruce. *Halfway to Heaven: The Hidden Life of the Carthusians*. 2nd ed. CS 186. Kalamazoo, MI: Cistercian Publications, 1999.

Louth, Andrew. "Apophatic and Cataphatic Theology." In *The Cambridge Companion to Christian Mysticism*, edited by Amy Hollywood and Patricia Z. Beckman. Cambridge: Cambridge University Press, 2012. 137–46.

Luxford, J. M., ed. *Studies in Carthusian Monasticism in the Late Middle Ages*. Turnhout: Brepols, 2008.

Miles, Laura Saetveit. "Richard Methley and the Translation of Vernacular Religious Writing in Latin." In *After Arundel: Religious Writing in Fifteenth-Century England*, edited by Vincent Gillespie and Kantik Ghosh. Turnhout: Brepols, 2011. 449–66.

Newman, Barbara. "Latin and the Vernaculars." In *The Cambridge Companion to Christian Mysticism*, edited by Amy Hollywood and Patricia Z. Beckman. Cambridge: Cambridge University Press, 2012. 225–39.

Renevey, Denis. "Name above Names: The Devotion to the Name of Jesus from Richard Rolle to Walter Hilton's *Scale of Perfection I*." In *The Medieval Mystical Tradition, England, Ireland, and Wales: Exeter Symposium VI*, edited by Marion Glasscoe. Cambridge: D. S. Brewer, 1999. 103–21.

———. " 'The Name Poured Out': Margins, Illuminations, and Miniatures as Evidence for the Practice of Devotions to the Holy Name of Jesus in Late Medieval England." In *The Mystical Tradition and the Carthusians,* vol. 9, edited by James Hogg. *Analecta Cartusiana* 130 (1996): 127–47.

Sargent, Michael. "Richard Methley." *Oxford Dictionary of National Biography*. Oxford, 2004. https://doi.org/10.1093/ref:odnb/69525.

———. "The Transmission by the English Carthusians of Some Late Medieval Spiritual Writings." *Journal of Ecclesiastical History* 27 (1976): 225–40.

Thompson, E. Margaret. *The Carthusian Order in England*. London: Society for Promoting Christian Knowledge, 1930.

Turner, Denys. *Eros and Allegory: Medieval Exegesis of the Song of Songs*. CS 156. Kalamazoo, MI: Cistercian Publications, 1995.

Voaden, Rosalynn. *God's Words, Women's Voices: The Discernment of Spirits in the Writing of Late-Medieval Women Visionaries*. York, UK: York Medieval Press, 1999.

Warren, Ann K. *Anchorites and Their Patrons in Medieval England*. Berkeley: University of California Press, 1985.

Windeatt, Barry. "1412–1534: Texts." In *The Cambridge Companion to Medieval English Mysticism*, edited by Vincent Gillespie and Samuel Fanous. Cambridge: Cambridge University Press, 2011. 195–224.

Zieman, Katherine. "Monasticism and the Public Contemplative in Late Medieval England: Richard Methley and His Spiritual Formation." *Journal of Medieval and Early Modern Studies* 42 (2012): 699–724.

Translator's Preface

Richard Methley, who was both a mystic and a connoisseur of mystical texts, is best known today for his translations from Middle English into Latin: *The Cloud of Unknowing* (*Divina caligo ignorantiae*) and Marguerite Porete's *The Mirror of Simple Souls* (*Speculum animarum simplicium*). But his original Latin works have never before been translated into English or any other tongue. There is good reason for this. Methley died in 1527/28, only seven years before the Dissolution, and most of his writings perished in the ensuing chaos. In the three and a half extant Latin texts presented in this volume, he mentions four others that do not survive: *The Cellar, On the Name of Mary and the Sacrament of the Altar, Three Ways of Excellence*, and *A Defense of the Solitary or Contemplative Life*.[1] However high the author's reputation may have stood in his lifetime, it was swiftly eclipsed by the Reformation.

The School of Languishing Love (1484), *The Bedroom of the beloved Beloved* (1485), and *The Refectory of Salvation* (1487) all appear in a single late fifteenth-century manuscript from Mount Grace Charterhouse: Cambridge, Trinity College O.2.56, written in two principal hands. M. R. James describes the manuscript in his catalogue as "most probably in the autograph of the author,"[2] and its numerous glosses and corrections do suggest a provenance

---

1. Their Latin titles are *Cellarium, De Marie nomine et sacramento altaris, Trivium excellencie*, and *Defensorium solitarie sive contemplative vite*.

2. M. R. James, *The Western Manuscripts in the Library of Trinity College, Cambridge*, vol. 3 (Cambridge: Cambridge University Press, 1902), 176.

close to him. However, as Laura Saetveit Miles notes in her Introduction, the colophon of *Refectory* indicates a different scribe at least for that work: "Here ends *The Refectory of Salvation*, composed from the most opulent drunkenness by that man of God, Richard Methley, filled with delights."

The hands are legible, though heavily abbreviated, but the Trinity manuscript does not present a particularly good text. A passage in *Refectory* helps to explain why. In chapter 37, Methley is praying (as he so often does) that he will soon die and join his Beloved in heaven. But the devil, he says, tempts him: "He told me I should not wish to be dissolved and be with Christ because I had books that I had corrected before, yet I came back to them later and found that something was still inaccurate—a word, a syllable, a letter, perhaps a title or something of that sort. So he said I should delay and correct them again." Methley rejects this advice as a temptation, arguing that if he were to die with his work unfinished, God would arrange for the correction of his books by some other means. The same text ends with a plea from the author to his readers, envisioned as potential copyists (chap. 41): "See, dearest brothers, I have written this *Refectory of Salvation* for you. Correct it if necessary, give thanks to God, and pray for me. If you have written well, correct what you have written; otherwise, I ask you not to write."

We learn from these anecdotes that the mystic did correct his own work and cared about producing an accurate text. Indeed, the Trinity manuscript reveals extensive corrections, including erasures as well as interlinear and marginal insertions. Yet many errors remain, often resulting in unclear or ungrammatical forms. Punctuation is sparse and at times misleading. Methley's editors, John Clark and James Hogg, supply numerous small emendations and faithfully record all scribal corrections in their apparatus. Regrettably, however, they do not succeed in resolving all the textual problems. For the purpose of translation, therefore, I have often had to emend the text, as well as making my own decisions about where sentences should begin and end. All chapter numbers and titles follow the manuscript, but the paragraph breaks are my own.

If Methley or anyone else ever made a fair copy of these three texts, it does not survive. Many of the scribal problems can be attributed to his working methods, for he wrote about his mystical experiences in "real time," snatching a few moments here and there after Mass, before Vespers, or whenever he could. He always scrupulously records the liturgical date as well as the time of day (within the cycle of the Office) for each of his experiences, and in each work he also mentions the year. Sometimes he explains exactly when he left off his writing and when he took it up again. All three works are addressed to his Carthusian brothers, an audience of seasoned contemplatives. He often refers to "the man of God" (*vir Dei* or *sanctus vir*), so I have preserved his masculine pronouns except in a few cases where he envisages humankind in general. Unlike Bernard of Clairvaux and others, Methley seldom speaks over the heads of his monks to address a wider audience. With rare exceptions, too, he does not bother to strive for eloquence. Instead, he writes an almost colloquial Latin, using a telescopic, elliptical style that counts on the intuitive grasp of those who knew him well and may have been familiar with his oral teaching. Some passages seem to have been written on the edge of ecstasy, such as the many chapters where he bursts into jubilant repetitions of the name of Jesus: *O Jesu Jesu Jesu! Jesu Jesu Jesu! Jesu Jesu Jesu!*

School, the first text in the manuscript, is the most systematic, offering instruction in contemplative prayer peppered with accounts of Methley's own revelations and experiences. It is also heavily glossed for teaching purposes, at least in part by the author himself, and presents the clearest text of the three. All the marginal glosses have been duly recorded by the editors and are included here as footnotes. *Refectory*, on the other hand, is a day-by-day spiritual diary, making only intermittent attempts to unify its meditations around a common theme. *Bedroom*, structured as a dialogue between Methley and Christ, falls somewhere in between. In the two latter texts, some passages are so obscure that the work of translation feels dangerously close to mind reading, requiring not only emendations but conjectures about what the author must have been thinking. I have been guided by similar, clearer passages elsewhere, and at several points I have checked the text by comparing the published edition with the manuscript.

Certain terms require special comment. For example, Methley often speaks of *amor sensibilis*. I have translated *sensibilis* consistently as "perceptible," its primary meaning, but the Latin is richer than the corresponding English term.[3] The related noun *sensus* can refer to the five senses but also to feelings, sensations, thoughts, sentiments, and meanings, while the verb *sentire* can mean "feel, see, perceive, experience, undergo, observe, understand, think, judge."[4] In Methley's usage, *sensibilis* always has a strong affective, experiential component. *Amor sensibilis* is love that is felt in the heart, perceived by the senses, experienced in the body. It is a gift for which aspiring contemplatives pray, while those who receive it express deep gratitude. Similarly, Methley speaks at times of a "spiritual sensation" (*sensacio*) that he receives during prayer. In *The Experience of Truth*, he names the presence of *amor sensibilis* as one of the chief criteria for determining whether a purported revelation is trustworthy.

Closely related to *amor sensibilis* is *amor languidus* or simply *languor*, inspired by the refrain of the Song of Songs: *quia amore langueo* (Song 2:5 and 5:8). Nearly every chapter of *School* ends with this refrain. I have rendered *amor languidus* as "languishing love" and *languor* by its English cognate, but readers should be aware that it also carries a sense of "sickness," especially fatigue or faintness. In *Bedroom* Methley uses the oxymoron of a sickly health or health-giving sickness, which will be familiar to readers of secular love poetry. *Quia amore langueo* is also the refrain of one of the most celebrated Middle English religious lyrics, "In

3. I thank Bernard McGinn for his advice on this problem.
4. *Sentio, sentire*, in D. A. Kidd, *Collins Gem Latin Dictionary* (London: William Collins, 1957).

the vaile of restles mynd," in which Christ himself languishes for love. In one of many wooing stanzas, he tells the narrator,

> I am treu love that fals was neuer,
> My sister, mannys soule, I loved hyr thus,
> Bycause I wold on no wyse disseuere
> I left my kyngdome gloriouse.
> I purueyd hyr a paleis preciouse.
> She flytt, I folowyd, I luffed hir soo
> That I suffred thes peynes piteuouse,
> *Quia amore langueo.*[5]

Methley was strongly influenced by Richard Rolle, a debt he acknowledges explicitly in *Refectory*, chapter 12: "my life consists of love, languor, sweetness, warmth, and song [*amore, languore, dulcore, feruore, canore*] . . . . The Beloved has promised me that I would experience love more often in languor, just as the kindly Richard of Hampole experienced it more often in warmth." All these rhyming Rollean terms occur often in Methley's work, but especially *languor* and *canor*. I have translated the latter as *song*, *music*, or *melody*, depending on context. Sometimes Methley calls it *canor angelicus*, the supreme gift of hearing angelic song and mentally joining in. No audible music is involved. But in certain passages, Methley imitates the intensely lyrical, alliterative style of Rolle's *Melos amoris*.[6] In *School*, chapter 12, for example, he writes, "mens mea . . . musicam multiplicat et merorem funditus fugauit a philomena, que filium et fratrem fulcitum floribus dulcissimum dilectum amplexatur in brachiis benediccionis." In such passages, which end as abruptly as they begin, the aural effect must take priority over the literal meaning. So I have

---

5. "In the vaile of restles mynd," stanza 3, in *Medieval Lyric: Middle English Lyrics, Ballads, and Carols*, ed. John C. Hirsh (Oxford: Blackwell, 2005), 58.

6. For a virtuosic translation, see *Richard Rolle's* Melody of Love: *A Study and Translation with Manuscript and Musical Contexts*, trans. Andrew Albin (Toronto: Pontifical Institute of Mediaeval Studies, 2018).

reproduced the alliteration as best I could: "My mind banishes mourning and multiplies music as God's nightingale embraces the bountiful Beloved, her brother and son, sustained by blossoms in the arms of his blessing."

A few technical terms of mystical or scholastic theology occur from time to time, such as *excessus mentis* (ecstasy), *sensualitas* (the body as a feeling, sensing, perceiving organism), and *scintilla syntheresis* (the apex or "spark" of the soul, which experiences divine union). In *School* Methley discusses what he calls *tedium*, a condition of world-weariness, boredom, and disgust that afflicts the monk when his devotion fails. The more familiar term for this in monastic literature is *acedia* (depression, sloth, sadness), but Methley never uses that word, perhaps because it designates one of the seven deadly sins and he does not want his monks to feel guilty when they suffer this affliction. I have rendered *tedium* as *ennui*, the French term being stronger than any English equivalent.

The title of *Bedroom* poses a special problem. Methley refers to Christ throughout his works as the Beloved, but in *Bedroom* he doubles that term. *Dilecti dilecti* occurs just once in the Vulgate (Ps 67:13), in what is certainly a mistranslation of the Hebrew: *Rex virtutum dilecti dilecti* (the King of virtues of the beloved Beloved). Methley picked up on the phrase to highlight the superlative quality of his love. In this amorous dialogue, he and Christ both address one another as "beloved Beloved," a term I have faithfully reproduced despite its peculiar ring in English.

Methley's fourth treatise, *The Experience of Truth*, stands apart from the others. This undated work, later than the rest, survives in a different manuscript: London, Public Record Office Collection SP 1/239. There the second half of this text (chap. 14 through the concluding chap. 27) precedes a short Middle English letter, *To hew heremyte—a pystyl of solytary lyfe nowadayes*. Although *Experience* still refers to the author's personal encounters with God, angels, and demons, it is primarily a treatise on the discernment of spirits, addressing such hot-button issues as how to determine the authenticity of a vision, how to respond to "the evangelists and prophets of modern times," how to advise a bishop who wants to exchange his pastoral duties for a contemplative life, and, perhaps most interesting, "what a holy man should do if he is asked to settle a dispute among theologians" (chap. 21). This suggests that Methley and his religious brothers sometimes found themselves in that situation. Unlike the other works, *Experience* concludes with an address to "sisters" as well as "fathers and brothers," and an anomalous passage on virginity.

I have noted all biblical allusions in the apparatus, with the exception that when Methley repeats a verse, as he frequently does, I mark only its first occurrence. Biblical passages are translated directly from the Vulgate. The apparatus also includes the dates of all saints' feasts mentioned in the text, citations and allusions to other medieval authors, occasional explanatory comments, and translations of all the marginal glosses in *School*.

Finally, I should note the surprising genesis of this translation, which is a fittingly contemplative one. In October 2018, the British Zen master Julian Daizan Skinner advertised on a Classics listserv, offering to pay for a translation of Methley's works to use in his meditation workshops. Intrigued by the notice, I sent for the recently published edition of Methley's *Works*, read them, and decided that this virtually unknown author deserved the attention of medievalists as well as Zen disciples. I would like to offer special thanks to Dr. Giuseppe Pezzini, lecturer in Latin at the University of St. Andrews, who answered Daizan Skinner's ad. We corresponded, and Dr. Pezzini, a specialist in Terence and ancient Roman comedy, very kindly sent me his draft translation of *Bedroom*. I found it helpful as I was beginning my work on this project, but the present translation is my own.

The School of Languishing Love

Here begins a prayer to introduce the book called
The School of Languishing Love.

O Jesus Christ, teacher of righteousness and lover of all who hope
in you, attend to the devout prayers of your servant, and grant that
I may so languish in your love[1] that for your love I may live and
die. As long as I live in this world, grant me special grace in praising you so that I may sing and burn in your love, really as well as
morally,[2] until you deign to give me what I await, namely yourself, in eternal life, with the Father and the Holy Spirit. Amen.

**Here ends the prayer. Here begins the prologue to
the aforesaid book.**

The highest aim of all creatures is to love and be loved,[3] but some
strive well and others badly to attain this goal. No one loves well
unless he loves the one God in Trinity and the Trinity in unity,
and loves all created things with due respect for God's sake.[4] For
this reason, because I love God with actual devotion (I give him

---

1. Song 2:5; this key verse is the refrain of the entire work.
2. *canam amore tuo et ardeam realiter et moraliter.* Like Richard Rolle in the
Incendium amoris (*The Fire of Love*), Methley speaks of a fire that is physical as well
as metaphorical. His theme of *canor* or spiritual song is also indebted to Rolle.
3. Cf. Augustine, *Confessions* II.2: "Et quid erat quod me delectabat, nisi amare
et amari?"
4. Augustine, *De doctrina christiana* (*On Christian Education*), 1.22.

thanks forever and ever), I try to arouse all people to love God. Because love is the cause of the whole universe, it can establish nothing better than love itself as a remedy, enabling everyone who wishes to love to attain at last to a perceptible love.[5]

It might seem difficult to see how this love, the best that exists, could be a remedy for the love of another. If you have ever loved an ungrateful person, you know what I mean.[6] But if you have never loved either God or an ingrate with perceptible love, then you do not yet know how love can be a remedy for love.[7] For love makes a person love someone else who does not return that love. If the beloved is willing and able to consider how painful unrequited love is, he will sooner fall in love because of the other's love than for any other reason, no matter what it may be.

I think the greatest of all pains is to love an ingrate.[8] But do not apply everything I have written to the enemy who must be loved.[9] No, you should understand that the person I am discussing torments the affectionate soul more than an enemy, even if he has inflicted no harm. Reason enjoins all good Christians to love their enemy for God's sake; yet that kind of love has little to do with affection. On the contrary, the kind of person I am discussing is loved freely and affectionately. In true lovers, the more such affection is rejected, the more it increases, or else it remains stable—

5. *amorem sensibilem*, a love that is both emotionally warm and perceptible to the senses. Methley uses the noun *amor* (rather than *dilectio* or *caritas*), but his preferred verb for loving is *diligere*.

6. *Marginal gloss:* "This means that everyone, however perfect, is still ungrateful to God in certain ways. So this whole analogy makes the point that we, who are ungrateful to God in many ways, may be roused to mutual love by the immensity of his gratuitous love."

7. *Marginal gloss:* "This is the meaning. When an ingrate is greatly loved by another, yet the beloved repays that love only with ingratitude, he may see that in spite of this, the other loves him no less. Thus he might be aroused to love him—even unwillingly, so to speak—by the constancy of the other's love."

8. The literature of courtly love, still flourishing in Methley's day, focused obsessively on unrequited love and the lover's suffering.

9. Matt 5:44; Luke 6:27.

provided that the lover is just as unchanging as God is.[10] In fact, such love can truly be ascribed to God alone. God therefore must be loved above all things. Because he is unchanging, a sinner who turns to him with his whole heart after his sin can firmly hope for love from the One whose love never changes.

That is not how it is among worldly people! What they love is not the goodness of a person's nature but the happiness of his fortune. Woe to those wretches, for they shall perish! But if I may use a human analogy, God, who knows what is secret and hidden, suffers the greatest pain because he loves an ingrate—that is, a human being who does not love him in return. And this is strange indeed, for God always loves and is always quick to be reconciled. Beyond all mortals or even immortals, it is he who can say "I languish for love." That is why this book, in keeping with its subject, is called *The School of Languishing Love*.

Here ends the prologue. Here begins the book called "The School of Languishing Love."

1. On love and languor, on fear and song, and on perceptible fire

"I languish for love." Experience teaches what it means to say "I languish for love," although it may seem like a contradiction that love involves languor when there should be delight in it. In languor, on the contrary, there is exasperation. But the knowledge of love, no doubt, can be perfectly acquired only by experience. Love is the most delightful thing there is, for it makes everyone in heaven rejoice eternally. To lovers of this world, languor is the most odious thing there is, for it snatches their delight and some-times even their life away. In this treatise, however, love and languor will be inseparable companions. Love is the cause of languor and languor the cause of love.

---

10. Persistence in unrequited love was understood as the supreme virtue of loyalty or constancy.

I would like to explain what love is and what this languor is—but I must ask for your attention. Where true love is concerned, no one can lose, so no one should hesitate to lend an ear. The kind of love we are discussing is both the cause and the reality of eternal bliss. Languor, though, is the remedy by which every rational creature can attain true love, without exception. This love is a condition of the soul that both wounds and heals.[11] It heals and wounds with perceptible delight, so that languor is the constant companion of love and love of languor. Indeed, languor is so full of love that even if the whole world were turned to joy, a person who languishes for love would not turn his eyes even once to see it. One who languishes like this cannot find gladness in anything except his beloved.[12]

No one who languishes for love of his Beloved can fear any creature. (You must understand that I refer to the relationship between God and man.) Blessed is he who languishes, for neither all the people in the world nor all the demons in hell can frighten him! The languor of love does not permit one who languishes to mourn. Instead, it compels a lover to sing. Love's languor produces fervent tears, and where there is fervor, there is sometimes a perceptible fire of love. The languor of love brings the man of God close to death—and this happens habitually. At such a time, absolutely nothing can make him afraid.[13] Any thought that occurs to his mind is transformed by the violence of his languor into a song of love.

One who languishes for the Beloved's love has no fear of his Judge's judgment. That is why he asks nothing of the Beloved

---

11. Cf. Job 5:18: *Quia ipse vulnerat et medetur.*

12. *Marginal gloss:* "All this applies to the love of God, not of the world or any other creature." Cf. Richard of St. Victor, *On the Four Degrees of Violent Charity* II.10. In the third degree of violent love (called *languidus amor*), "nothing besides the beloved can satisfy the mind."

13. *Marginal gloss:* "For perfect love casts out fear." 1 John 4:18.

except death.[14] Yet he often receives from him what he does not ask, that is, something that is better in its time. Because he loves and languishes, he suffers pain, yet at the same time he is sweetly filled with the fullest delights[15]—and he says, "I languish for love."

2. On love and languor; how even God himself languishes, in a way, and how a human does

The languor of love can be understood in many ways, both good and bad.[16] I intend that all should know it in a good way; may the love of the Beloved grant this! Our God, who is Love itself,[17] languishes for love because he is good. He also languishes for love because he loves an ingrate who does not return his love. Again, he languishes for love because he is waiting for someone who does love him—waiting to crown him in due time. Undoubtedly, he languishes with the noblest love because he calls a person who turns away from him to return—yet he pays no attention to someone who formerly loved him.[18] He languishes for love too, because he never ceases to offer his passion for those who repent.

A human being languishes for love because, when his devotion runs dry, he is gravely afflicted by ennui. He languishes for love because, for a long while, he never ceases to desire that his affection might become sweeter, and this does not happen. No doubt this is because he is not paying perfect attention, or else the time

14. A major theme of *The Bedroom of the beloved Beloved* and *The Refectory of Salvation.*

15. *Marginal gloss:* "The languor of love, though sweet, is painful because of the Beloved's delay, for hope deferred afflicts the soul." Prov 13:12.

16. This chapter supplies a table of contents for the rest of the treatise.

17. *ipse amor est.* Cf. 1 John 4:8, *Deus caritas est.*

18. *Marginal gloss:* "This sentence agrees with a certain saint's remark in the person of Christ: 'Greater than all my pain is my inner suffering because I find you ungrateful.' But it should be noted that no suffering can befall God; that is impossible. Because of the weakness of human understanding, however, God is said by analogy with humans to languish, suffer pain, feel hatred, and similar things."

of his affection has not yet come.[19] He languishes for love because, even though he experiences love with the greatest delight, it torments him beyond everything that he does not yet see the Beloved. He languishes for love because he unites his will perfectly with the will of the Beloved. Because he does this voluntarily, he experiences the greatest languor. He languishes for love because it is tiresome for him to remain alive for even one moment. He languishes for love because he fears to be held back from the Beloved even after death—a delay he can scarcely endure.[20] If it seemed that even in Paradise, in the empyrean heaven, he could be satisfied by some lesser good than God, he would not believe it, for he languishes vehemently for love. Finally, a person languishes for love because of the mighty struggle between the spirit and the flesh.[21] The spirit constantly yearns to depart at once, yet the flesh desires the opposite. And so I say, "I languish for love."

3. On faithfulness between the lover and the Beloved; who is a thief and who is a robber; and that a person should entrust himself to the Beloved

The first lesson for anyone who wants to feel the languor of love is to have faith in the fidelity of the Beloved. He should have such perfect confidence in that fidelity[22] that he is ready to live and die

19. *Marginal gloss:* "By a secret dispensation of God, it very often happens that perceptible affection is delayed. But the virtue of love nevertheless remains if someone perseveres in good will and intention."

20. Methley here (and elsewhere) echoes Margery Kempe, whose *Book* is preserved only in a manuscript from Mount Grace. Kempe says that she "wept ful plenteuowsly . . . for desyr of the blys of hevyn and for sche was so long dyfferryd therfro," but Christ tells her that "sche schuld abyden and languren in lofe." *The Book of Margery Kempe*, ed. Lynn Staley (Kalamazoo, MI: Medieval Institute, 1996), 34, chap. 7.

21. Cf. Gal 5:17; Eph 6:12.

22. Cf. 1 John 4:17.

before he knowingly[23] takes pleasure in a creature[24]—unless it increases his affection for the Beloved. But that rarely happens in the perfect, and indeed, they are still imperfect until they freely love the Beloved for his own sake. This fidelity teaches a person to keep his mind free at all times,[25] not just on some schedule.[26]

Some people may find this strange, so I will explain more fully. Affection prompts every lover to love the Beloved freely for his own sake, because he sees such abundant signs of his love all around him. Anyone who loves with an ulterior motive proves that he loves not God himself, but his goods. So he is no true lover of God but (if I may say so) a thief and a robber.[27] If he could have whatever he loves without God's knowledge, he would care nothing for God's love—and this causes God the greatest pain because he loves an ingrate. (I am speaking in a human way here. When we attribute a human passion to God, it is the figure of anthropomorphism.)[28]

If you love God freely, as I said, have faith that he cannot possibly abandon you for long. To the extent that you are faithful, by his grace you will experience his faithfulness just as much and incomparably more, for God has no measure. See who is at fault, then, if you are troubled! It is your own fault because you do not show fidelity, and that in turn is because you do not perfectly

23. *Marginal gloss:* "*Knowingly* means deliberately and with full intention. Otherwise, if this happens from weakness or in the assault of temptation, it does not altogether impede the perfection of love. For the righteous falls seven times in a day." Prov 24:16.

24. *Marginal gloss:* "In reason, that is, even though the sensuality may grumble and resist."

25. *Marginal gloss:* "To understand at all times with a good and unimpaired will, free of all earthly love, all carnal affection, and desire for any kind of pleasure or consolation, except in God or for God's sake."

26. *semper non horatim.*

27. John 10:8.

28. *Antropaspathos. Marginal gloss:* "*Antropaspathos* is when a human passion is attributed to God, such as saying that God is angry or rejoices, etc. This figure is very common in the Scriptures."

believe in him. You do not believe because you do not have perceptible love.[29] Further, you do not have perceptible love because
you busy yourself pointlessly with transitory things.[30]

Here is what you should do. If you can find it in your heart to
be perfect and sell or abandon all transitory things,[31] entrust yourself to the Beloved like the ancient fathers,[32] as it is handed down
in writing. When you have done this, entrust yourself once again
to the Beloved in all contingencies. Note that I said *all* contingencies, however they arise—from humans, the devil, or the flesh.[33]

You ask, "How should I entrust myself to the Beloved?"

I say, "Tell him this: 'I languish for love because I have no love;
I am weak in virtues because I feel no love. To you, my Beloved,
I entrust all care for myself.[34] As for me, I am poor and needy.[35]
But as for you, take care of me! Make me languish perceptibly
for your love, I pray, so that just as you are my faithful lover, I
may be your faithful lover—until at last I can say with supreme
thanksgiving, for your honor and the salvation of all people, I
languish for love.' "

29. *Marginal gloss:* "There is a certain kind of faith in the perfect called 'formed
faith,' which is a perceptible contact with divinity. It is much more excellent and
efficacious than ordinary faith, and cannot be attained except through perceptible
love."

30. *Marginal gloss:* "You busy yourself pointlessly (*supervacue*), that is, idly and
in vain, because no good fruit comes of this. For a monk, any occupation with transitory things is pointless and idle unless it occurs through obedience, charity, or
necessity."

31. Matt 19:21; Mark 10:21; Luke 18:22.

32. *Marginal gloss:* "Like the ancient fathers: this means to entrust body and soul
purely and simply to God, and to a human being (that is, a superior) for God's sake."

33. *Marginal gloss:* "They can arise from humans through external losses in
property or reputation, through scandal or abuse, slander, or anything of that kind
that can happen. They can arise from the devil through hidden suggestions and
temptations, or from the flesh through its shameful and rebellious motions."

34. 1 Pet 5:7.

35. Ps 39:18.

4. How God works in a human being; of required and voluntary exercises; and of a peaceful mind

If you do these things, O mortal, what you cannot accomplish by yourself without serious difficulty, he will accomplish by himself (because he languishes for love) or else through another (because he is great in honor).[36] What is more,[37] even if you can get your work done without serious difficulty,[38] you will do it through him, for it is he who works within you both to will and to act.[39] Without him you can do nothing,[40] so in a way he does everything in you and for your sake.

I want you to understand here that you will accomplish all the duties you need to carry out,[41] whether for the sake of obedience, your physical needs, or brotherly love. Even if you were ravished into heaven at the time, I know that God would either provide for the task some other way or else calm your languishing love. Do not worry about the future or the past. If it is not yet time for you to remember something, entrust yourself to the Beloved and say, "I do not know the outcome of things uncertain, but I am bound to love God with all my heart."[42] When the time comes for you to attend to anything, ask God for help. Whatever you can achieve with a peaceful conscience, it will go well with you and the task at hand. As for what you cannot do, seek counsel, or if necessary, entrust it to the judgment of your superiors. Then you can rest in

---

36. *Marginal gloss:* "According to this verse [Ps 36:5], 'reveal your way to the Lord and hope in him, and he will do it,' either by himself or by some other means."

37. MS *Quod autem minus est*; reading *maius* for *minus*.

38. *Marginal gloss:* "For we are fellow workers with God, so we must do what is in us and whatever we can by human effort (with the help of grace), not leaving it all to God—for that would be to tempt God." Cf. Deut 6:16; Luke 4:12; 1 Cor 3:9.

39. Phil 2:13.

40. John 15:5.

41. *Marginal gloss:* "For the Holy Spirit does not take anything we do kindly if we have neglected what we are bound to do."

42. Deut 6:5; Luke 10:27.

peace with the Beloved, saying in your heart or your affection, "I languish for love."

5. A disputation and complaint of God against ungrateful humanity

"I languish for love," says the Lord God, "and in perpetual charity I have loved you."[43] O man, do not be ungrateful to your God![44] Because I am good, I created you.[45] Because I am good, I made you good. Because I am good, I made you to be loved. Because I am good, I disposed you to enjoy me, the supreme good. Because I am good, I languish for love on your account. Because I am good, I created you to praise me where you can always have love, and never have painful languor.[46] O man, I languish for love on your account, for your ingratitude crucifies me. O man, I languish for love!

Hear me in my surpassing languor, I beg you, and I will teach you to be ungrateful to your lover no more. Because I am good, you are given a choice. Please, man, I beg you: deign to love me, for I languish for love. Love compels me to give you a choice of whether you want to be damned or saved, but where I find you, there I will judge you.[47] So because I am good, I give counsel, I promise mercy, I blissfully offer eternal life—for I languish for love.

---

43. Jer 31:3.

44. *Marginal gloss in Hand B:* "Nothing displeases God so much as ingratitude, especially in the children of grace (that is, religious people). For it blocks up the paths of grace, and where there is ingratitude, grace has no access and finds no place."

45. This complaint is indebted to Ps 135 with its refrain, "*Confitemini Domino, quoniam bonus, / Quoniam in aeternum misericordia eius.*" (Confess to the Lord, for he is good, for his mercy endures forever.)

46. *Marginal gloss in Hand B:* "God made humankind for himself, not because he needed man, but that he might give himself to man to enjoy, for there was no better gift he could give him. For God wanted to be served by man so that, by means of that service, not God but man the servant would be helped, and he wanted the world to serve man so that man might likewise be helped by that means."

47. *Ubi te invenero, ibi te iudicabo.* A legal maxim; it means that jurisdiction may be asserted over a person whenever he or she is found in the territory of the judicial body.

O man, what better thing can you desire than to love? Because I am good, love me and you will have me, for I languish for love. What has displeased you in me so that you do not love me—I, who created you for my love? If you wanted to love me truly, you would have no toil.[48] If you wanted to love just as I do, you would rejoice forever, for on your account I languish for love. Sorrow will cease when love comes, for I languish for love. It is impossible for you to grow weary if you deign to keep faith with your beloved.[49] I myself languish for love, so you need not despair of your beloved. If you come, I will meet you; if you delay, I will wait for you. If you cry out, I am near, for I languish for love. I beg, I pray, I knock, I beseech, I adjure you![50] Please reciprocate, for I languish for love.

O man, all that I have suffered for you is little next to your ingratitude.[51] This is what crucifies me! This tortures me, this scourges me—for I languish for love. Because I am good, I will wait for you. Because I am good, I will inspire repentance.[52] Because I am good, I will increase my indulgence. Because I am good, when you come to me in true love I will embrace you, and when you die I will crown you. Because I am good, I will raise you from the dead. Because I am good, I will grant you to reign with me eternally.

Because I am good, I will now give you an example of loving. Think as best you can of how freely I loved you—for, because I am good, I loved you in my foreknowledge even before you

---

48. *Marginal gloss:* "Because all things are sweet and easy to a lover."

49. *Marginal gloss:* "Because God supplies either sweetness or patience."

50. Cf. Matt 7:7; Song 2:7.

51. *Marginal gloss:* "For nothing so displeases God as sin; again, nothing so tortures God as our ingratitude, according to what is said above: 'all that I have suffered for you is little.'"

52. *Marginal gloss:* "From his pure goodness he does whatever good he does for us, with no merits on our part. So, because he is good, he both inspires repentance in us and grants indulgence and remission of sins, bestows grace, etc., doing all of this freely beyond a doubt."

existed.[53] When you did not yet exist and could give me nothing, I freely loved you. When I created you, you had nothing of yourself except through me.[54] I gave you everything if only you would love me; therefore I loved you freely. You were a faithless lover, for you fell—so by not loving me, you lost everything and deserved to die. Therefore when I restored you, I freely loved you, for you had nothing that you could give me. Afterward you despised me by sinning actually, or at least mentally, and thus you deserved to be damned and once again lost everything. So, because I inspired you to repentance and reconciled you to me in confession, I freely loved you. See then that I languish for love! O man, be ungrateful to your God no longer—for I languish for love.

6. The analogy of a grateful lover and an ungrateful beloved. A person who desires to love God should have a great and holy desire, because no one is his equal.

The second reason Christ languishes for love is that he loves an ingrate, one who does not return his love.[55] You lovers—whoever you are, whatever your condition: my discourse will be about the languor of love, so speak from what you know in your heart. What is more painful than to love an ingrate? We can prove this from the opposite case. If you love someone who loves you back, you will bear everything gratefully for your lover's love. Indeed, some people even die for the man or woman they love, like those who perish in

---

53. *Marginal gloss:* "As it is written, 'In perpetual charity I have loved you, etc.'" Jer 31:3.

54. *Marginal gloss:* "According to the Apostle's saying, 'What do you have that you did not receive?'" 1 Cor 4:7.

55. *Marginal gloss in Hand B:* "It is a disgrace to you if your ingratitude stems from vices and pernicious sins. What so obviously impedes the working of grace as ingratitude? Over the course of time, we often grow lukewarm from the fervor of our initial conversion. Then charity gradually grows cold and wickedness easily abounds [Matt 24:12], so that we who began in the fervor of the spirit may end in the pleasures of the flesh."

wars or duels. It is clear that love makes everything easy, wherever it is found—in a boyfriend or girlfriend, even a sugar daddy or a mistress.[56] On the other hand, what is more bitter than to suffer so much for an ingrate? Doubtless you know what I mean, whether you are a spiritual lover or a carnal one. Nothing hurts a lover so much as ingratitude, so God is right to complain about man and say, "I languish for love, because my love is unrequited."

O man, you were naturally created for loving! Do not pervert the mode of your creation. As you were created to love the supreme good, which is God, never stop seeking and knocking, begging and weeping,[57] that divine goodness may bestow on you the special gift of love. Above all creatures—so far as it is possible, fitting and right—you should love him freely, for he freely created you as an amorous creature. In this way you will excel in everything you do, so as not to stain your glory. To invite you to this goal, God says to you, "I languish for love."

7. On the vehemence of love and languor experienced by the author of this book on the feast of Saint Peter in Chains

The languor of love is ineffable, yet if we said nothing about it, some might say it does not exist at all. So, God willing, I will explain what I have learned from experience in my small degree. Even if I cannot expound it as it truly is,[58] have no doubt that what I am going to say is true. Just because an experienced person teaches,[59] thanks to God, the inexperienced should not slander the hermit out of envy.

---

56. *in amato vel amica, fautore seu amasia. Marginal gloss:* "An *amasia* [mistress] is a woman whom someone loves in vice."

57. Cf. Matt 7:7.

58. *sicuti est.* Cf. 1 John 3:2.

59. *expertus docet.* Cf. the hymn "Iesu dulcis memoria": *Expertus potest credere / Quid sit Iesum diligere* (One who has experienced it can believe what it is to love Jesus).

On the feast of Saint Peter in Chains, [60] I was physically in the church at Mount Grace. After the Mass I had celebrated, as I was giving thanks to God in meditation and prayer, God visited me with great power: I languished so vehemently for love that I almost died. I will tell you how this happened, my brothers, as best I can by the grace of God. The love and desire of the Beloved received me into heaven in spirit until I lacked nothing (so far as I know) of the glory of God who sits on the throne,[61] except for death itself.[62] Then I forgot all pain and fear and had no thought of anything, even the Creator, or at least no deliberate thought.

When people are alarmed by a dangerous fire, they do not shout, "Fire has attacked my house, come and help me!" In their anguish, not to say agony, they can hardly utter a word. So they just shout "Fire, fire, fire!" Or if the spirit moves them even more powerfully, they scream "Ah, ah, ah!"—and they mean by that sound to express their danger. So it was with me, in my small way.[63] At first I kept commending my spirit to God by saying "Into your hands," [64] either vocally or (as I suspect) mentally. But as the languor of love grew more intense, I could hardly think and I only formed in my spirit the word *Amor, Amor, Amor!* Love, love, love![65] Finally, as I fell away from even that formula; I waited for the moment when I could totally breathe forth my spirit. Then I could only sing (rather than shout) *Ah, ah, ah*, or something like that, in my spiritual joy.

---

60. August 1, 1484.

61. Rev 3:21, 4:9.

62. *Marginal gloss:* "For the corruptible body vexes the soul, and the earthly dwelling oppresses the mind that thinks of many things." Wis 9:15.

63. *Marginal gloss:* "For the fervor of love very often takes even the lover's voice away."

64. Luke 23:46.

65. Cf. *The Cloud of Unknowing*, chap. 7 (on the word *love*) and chap. 38 (the example of a fire). Methley translated this work into Latin under the title *Divina caligo ignorancie*.

O lovers, now you must know how I languish for love and truly desire to be dissolved and be with Christ.[66] Glory to him forever! He has given me the gift of humility and brotherly love, and so I languish for love.

8. On learning about languor from signs and from experience; on the preparation for learning; and on very frequent rapture

Christ languishes because of delay, for he waits patiently to crown his lover in due time—the very best time, no doubt. How can anyone understand how love languishes in delay unless he has learned to love? There are many signs that reveal a person's great love for another. But someone who has experienced love's delay learns more in a moment than someone else learns from these signs in a lifetime.[67] Yet what of that? Just because you are still ignorant, does that mean you cannot learn to love? Or because you have not yet experienced it, should you blush to learn? Experience is given by God, but the way to it is paved with righteousness. So learn from the signs how God languishes for love, waiting to crown his beloved with glory and honor[68] in great and marvelous sweetness, and sometimes even with angelic song.[69]

What are these signs? The signs of love are the frequent raptures experienced by the man of God—unitive and ecstatic rapture. And what happens in the fire of rapture if not the embrace and the

---

66. Song 2:5; Phil 1:23.

67. *Marginal gloss:* "A person is seriously tested by love's delay to see whether he is faithful in love, for no pain is so severe for a lover as not to feel the presence of his beloved. So a person learns more about love from the delay of the loved object than from other signs. For holy desires (as Gregory says) grow by delay." *Hand B adds:* "if the desires fade because of delay, they were not holy." See Gregory I, *Homiliae in Evangelia* 25.2 and *Moralia in Job* 26.XIX.34.

68. Ps 8:6. A note at the foot of the page reads "Note thus in Bonaventure, fol. 115, 2, partis a."

69. *in multo et mirifico dulcore, immo aliquando angelico canore.* The language (complete with internal rhyme) is reminiscent of Rolle.

union of love?[70] "For I languish for love," as the Beloved says to the beloved. It is true beyond the shadow of a doubt that God would never ravish and unite a mortal to himself in this way, so very often, unless he himself languished for love on account of his surpassing charity. So the hermit has great hope and desire to be dissolved when he learns from such signs that his Beloved loves him. He languishes for his part as if he could scarcely wait for the day of his death. Yet the Beloved very often—and I mean very, *very* often—ravishes the mortal into his surpassingly lovely light, as if to say not only in deed, but even in words, "I languish for love."

9. On the one who languishes for love of God; on patience; and on one who can neither feel envy nor be damned

God also languishes for love because, when someone turns away from him, he calls that person back and receives him with great mercy if he comes. Yet he pays no attention to that wretch who formerly loved the Beloved, the most sweet Jesus Christ, the only-begotten Son of God. Learn patience from this, brothers! If someone turns away from you in anger, though he was once a beloved friend, you should not cast him off, despise him, or despair of him. Rather, you should call him back.[71] It is fitting for you to wait, because almighty God waits, languishing for love. He does not pine away in anger or hatred, but acts like an infant a few days old,[72] who knows nothing of injury and ingratitude. If anyone behaves differently, I am absolutely certain (no matter who objects) that if he says "I languish for love," he is lying.

---

70. *Marginal gloss in Hand B:* "Sometimes love causes a new, perceptible change in a person which makes reason cry out, sensing the presence of the Beloved, 'this is true love'—and consent to it."

71. Cf. Aelred of Rievaulx, *De spiritali amicitia* (*On Spiritual Friendship*), 3.15–25.

72. Isa 65:20.

No one who languishes for love can possibly envy his brother. Christ calls him back—and how can you know? Because he does not at once condemn him. It is a sign of the greatest goodness that even when the Almighty condemns, he does not wish to damn a person at once. Instead, he waits. This patience surely proceeds from love, and the proof is that God needs nothing, just as the prophet says: "For you have no need of my goods."[73] So love is the reason he waits. From this you can understand how he says to you, "I languish for love."

Yet if he punishes a sin at once and inspires repentance, that is an even surer sign that he languishes for love. If you are truly penitent, you absolutely cannot be damned—that is, if you die in that state. So God certainly languishes for love, whether he chastises or patiently waits. As for you, do not be ungrateful and procrastinate, but do penance at once and say, "O Lord, have mercy, have mercy, for I languish for love." You are languishing if you are *not* loving! But love's languor is caused sometimes by its absence, sometimes by its presence.[74] Say therefore, "I languish for love."

10. An analogy for the building of the church and religious life. How the death of Christ is frequently repeated. On the life of a person who cries out, Bah!

Fifth, Christ languishes for love because he never ceases to offer his passion for penitents. Who can understand how much pain he

---

73. Ps 15:2. *Marginal gloss in Hand B:* "O Lord, you know that I have nothing of myself, except what you have bestowed on me through union and the merits of your passion."

74. *Marginal gloss:* "Languor from the absence of love is when the soul is afflicted by ennui from the lack of perceptible love and the Beloved's absence. Languor from the presence of love is when the soul faints from the fervor of perceptible love because of the greatness of its desire when it cannot fully grasp what it longs for, according to this verse: 'My soul faints with desire in the courts of the Lord. My heart and my flesh have exulted in the living God.' Ps 83[:3]."

suffered on the cross in his passion? It surpasses all pain and sorrow, as he says himself: "All you who pass by, attend and see if there is any pain like my pain."[75] Rightly then he cries out and says, "I languish for love."

Think of a king seated on his throne with the whole earth subject to him. When he intends to build a castle, he summons his wise men from all sides. With their counsel and labor, he fulfills the plans he had first conceived in his heart. When the construction is finished, people say, "the king built this"—even though he never set his hand to the work. How then did he build it, if not that he was its cause? In the same way Christ, who is the Wisdom of the Father[76] dwelling in heaven, to whom all power has been given in heaven and on earth,[77] decided to build a castle of love and finished it, for love is strong as death.[78] He summoned his wise men from all sides, though it was he himself who gave them wisdom.[79] With the counsel and labor that he inspired in them, he fulfilled his plans. The construction was finished when the religious life was perfected and fully established. And because he is the cause, he himself built it through the holy fathers. It is obvious, then, that this king is Christ. The castle is religious life, the wise men are the doctors of the church, and the cause no doubt is that he languishes for love. In this building he never ceases to offer his passion for penitents. Thanks to him forever and ever! I mean that he offers it in the celebration of Masses, and therefore without ceasing (to speak broadly).[80]

75. Lam 1:12.

76. 1 Cor 1:24.

77. Matt 28:18.

78. Song 8:6. Cf. Robert Grosseteste's allegory, *Le Chasteau d'Amour* (*The Castle of Love*).

79. *Marginal gloss in Hand B:* "Not the wisdom of this world [1 Cor 1:20], which busies the heart with sly devices, cloaks its meaning in words, holds out lies as truths, and makes truths out to be lies." Cf. Gregory, *Moralia in Job* 10.XXIX.48.

80. *Marginal gloss:* "Because this happens daily, not continually."

Ungrateful man, why do you pay no attention to the one who
died for you, who has so often recently hung on the cross?[81] He
languishes for love on the altar in your presence, perhaps while
you are serving or even celebrating. Yet you treat him with no
reverence at all, and (what is worse) with no compassion. He says
"I languish for love," and you say, "I will kill you!" How can this
be, if not that you are the cause of his death? As long as you are
ungrateful, so long you are in some way the cause of his death.
His one-time death on the cross is over,[82] yet a person who continues to live without gratitude crucifies him more than once.[83]
Christ caused the building of his church and holy religion—and
you cause its destruction. He gave his blood for you, and you give
your whole way of life against him. He possesses all things in
abundance except your heart, which he continually desires. And
you dare to answer him, "Bah!"[84] Your whole life utters this cry!
Your life blasphemes him, your life takes arms against him—and
yet you dare to present yourself before so great a judge. Now he
says, "I languish for love."[85] But later he will say "Where I find
you, there I judge you"—and he will do it.[86]

11. How man cures the ailing Christ, and a prayer to Christ

O man, do not be ungrateful to your Maker! Go to the crucifix
and set him free. Heal his hands, his feet, and his side, for you are

81. *Marginal gloss:* "For that sacred host is sacrificed daily on the altar and offered
for sins."

82. *Marginal gloss:* "In the body, that is." Cf. Rom 6:10; Heb 7:27; 1 Pet 3:18.

83. *Marginal gloss:* "According to the Apostle's saying, 'Crucifying the Son of
God for themselves once again,' etc." Heb 6:6.

84. *Vath,* a vernacular exclamation of contempt. *Marginal gloss:* "That is, with
indignation and contempt, for sinning shows contempt for God. Every sinner (at least
one who sins mortally) despises God."

85. *Marginal gloss:* "For this is the place and time for love and mercy; hereafter
there will be strict justice."

86. Legal maxim; see note 47 above.

a physician. Perhaps you deny it or blush that I call you one—but listen patiently. He says, "I languish for love." See, he languishes for your love! If he languishes for your love, then give it to him and he will have what he yearns for. Carnal lovers languish until they attain what they desire. But once they have it, they are not only healed; they glory in their medicine for the rest of their lives. Then won't Christ insist all the more that he is healed and glory in it? Yes indeed! That is how, if you are a lover, you are a physician.[87] And where will you hide yourself if you do not heal the Son of God while you can? As you well know, all schemes against him are in vain.[88]

Therefore, man, do not flee, but take refuge in him and say in solemn prayer, "Lord Jesus Christ, my lover, you languish in love for me. Trusting in your mercy, I come to you and lay my prayer at your feet. You languish for love and seek love from me. I don't doubt that what you request would please you. But as for me, I don't have it, for I know that what you ask is your own gift. If you ask me for something I don't have unless you give it, and then you don't deign to give, whose fault will it be if you go away empty? Because I know that you are kind, generous, and merciful, I have found the courage to ask for what you in turn ask of me. I cannot doubt that it will give you great pleasure to do everything for love. So I will lack nothing if I love you,[89] but nothing could help me if I leave you.

"Love is the cause of everything. If I possess all things in you, I will glory securely; if I lose all things without you, I will wander the world in vain. So I will necessarily return to you and find you to be a gracious giver. If love can somehow take you down from

87. Jesus himself is often represented as a physician of souls; cf. Matt 9:12-13. But Methley borrows a topos of courtly love derived from Ovid, in which the beloved (usually a woman) is the only physician who can heal her languishing lover.

88. *Marginal gloss:* "For no power can prevail against the Lord; none can hide from his heat." Ps 18:7.

89. *Marginal gloss in Hand B:* "I will lack nothing if I love, etc. Take note."

the cross and heal you, and you yourself can supply that gift, I am sure that love is what I need above all—so I ask for love. I offer love in return, and I yearn to languish for love! I desire to be released from the body in love for your perpetual praise and the salvation of all the faithful, living and dead. O Jesus Christ, my lover, truly the teacher of righteousness, you languish for love. To every sinner and penitent, you constantly say through your actions, 'I languish for love. Have mercy on me, for you crucify me all day and all night.' To you be supreme thanksgiving forever and ever! For I languish for love."

12. *On overcoming ennui, and on an experience of union*

In the sixth place, we must explain how someone languishes for love when devotion runs dry. He is afflicted with terrible ennui all the day long.[90] It is hard for anyone to understand a discourse on love unless he has experienced it. So if you lack devotion, pay close attention and listen to me.

I myself was once tested by ennui, but if I remember well, I have never been overcome by it from the time I entered the hermitage until now. I have completed seven years here, and this is my eighth, as I write these things for you in the hermitage of Mount Grace on the day before the feast of Saint Oswald the King.[91] Because I am a Carthusian, I invite you to the same profession. Thanks to the Beloved, I have overcome ennui and obtained superabundant joy. I have kept the faith; I have persevered; I have found what I sought.[92] Follow me, or rather Christ in me,[93] and I promise that you too will find what I have found.

90. Latin *tedium* (boredom, weariness, disgust, loathing) is a strong term. In monastic literature it is related to the sin of *acedia* (sloth tinged by depression), which can make a monk flee from his cell in horror.
91. This feast fell on August 5, 1484.
92. Matt 7:7; 2 Tim 4:7.
93. 1 Cor 4:16; 11:1.

I was tested by the most terrible ennui to the point where, even though I was very firm in faith, I felt as if my whole body were falling away from its joints. If I remember well, I could barely hold myself up with a staff. If it had not been for a rumor about me (for I refused to have it said that I was sick), I would have lain in bed crying to God, "I languish for love!" Before this time I had been drenched in tears—rebaptized, in a way. But now it pleased the Beloved to test me, to see if I truly loved him or only his gifts, so he took away what he had given before. Left poor and desolate in the desert, I cried out, "I languish for love!" He was undoubtedly present, just as he had once been for Saint Anthony. But he waited to see my struggle[94] and gave me the grace of perseverance—because it pleased him, not because I deserved it, even if I achieved great things.

Afterward, because he found me faithful and great-hearted, he doubled his gifts in me. Thanks be to him forever and ever! Before, I used to weep for my own sins and the sins of others, and I had great hope of the heavenly kingdom. But since he languishes for love, when he saw me in so much pain that I almost died of fervor, he doubled his gifts this way with sweetness. He changed my tears into melody, for now I already sing with the angels. United with God (though its natural substance remains),[95] my mind banishes mourning and multiplies music as God's nightingale[96] embraces the bountiful Beloved,[97] her brother and son, sustained by blossoms in the arms of his blessing.[98] My hope,

---

94. Cf. Athanasius, *Life of St. Anthony*, chap. 10.

95. The "natural substance" of the mind remains intact, i.e., the distinction between Creator and creature is maintained even in mystical union—a safeguard against heresy.

96. *Marginal gloss:* "That is, the devout soul of the one who writes these things." John of Howden (fl. 1269–1275) wrote a lengthy devotional poem, *Philomena* (*The Nightingale*), which also influenced Rolle.

97. *Marginal gloss:* "That is, Jesus."

98. Song 2:5. Both Methley's thought and the alliteration recall Rolle's *Melos amoris* (*Melody of Love*).

too, is largely changed to fulfillment.[99] One thing alone I ask every day in solemn prayer: because I am filled with overwhelming joy, may God graciously call me out of this world with his holy summons—for himself, through himself, and to himself,[100] by every good means, so far as it is possible, fitting and right—for I languish for love. When I say "I languish," I do not mean because of the delay, but in every moment, because vehement love knows no reason.[101]

One part of this matter remains to be told. But I can scarcely grasp it in my own thoughts; how much less can I put it in words or in writing? Yet, by the grace of the Beloved, I will not keep silent about what little I can express. So I beg you, pay attention, for brotherly zeal compels me to speak. In union with Jesus Christ, I do all my work and offer to God the Father all I do in my life, as if to say in prayer or meditation, "This Mass, this prayer—with all respect for the intentions of the Church and the order—is especially for me,[102] so far as it is possible, fitting and right, by every good means, in union with our Lord Jesus Christ your Son, and every creature with him in its proper place.[103] Let it be as if Christ himself were speaking or celebrating Mass with his own mouth, with all who are united with him in such a union, for as many times as there are creatures in heaven, earth, and purgatory, for

---

99. *Spem . . . mutavit in rem.*

100. *Propter seipsum, per seipsum, ad seipsum.* The phrasing recalls the Canon of the Mass. *Marginal gloss:* "For himself, because he is the cause of our salvation; through himself, because he is the way by which we go; to himself, because he is the life to which we go."

101. *Marginal gloss:* "For vehement love always desires to be dissolved and be with Christ." Phil 1:23.

102. *Marginal gloss:* "Because charity always begins with oneself, as it is written: 'To have mercy on your own soul is pleasing to God.'" *Hand B adds:* Ecclesiasticus 30 [Sir 30:24].

103. *Marginal gloss:* "Understand every rational creature. Thus he includes all people without exception in this universal intention." Cf. *The Bedroom of the beloved Beloved*, chap. 14.

each and all of them, from the first to the last." This is my intention, brothers, in my small measure, so far as I can write it. Yet I
feel much more in my mind than I am able to say.[104] Love without
limits has given me a desire without limits—so I languish for love.

13. On ennui, on faithfulness, and on perseverance in free love

You too, sluggish one, if you want perceptible devotion, then have
it—or at least have a devout intention to attain what you desire.
If I'm not mistaken, nothing helps more to achieve prayer than to
have such an intention. But faith—where is your faith? Without
faith in the Beloved, no one can possibly feel love's languor.[105] I
have explained this before, but I am compelled in charity to say
a little more here. If you direct your intention freely toward God,
as you should—that is, if you seek to have him, enjoy him, praise
him, and love him for his own sake because he is good—it is impossible for him not to care for you.[106] Whatever you need for
your salvation, I promise that he will provide for you, giving it to
you either directly with no great difficulty, or through someone
else. So let your mind hold firmly to what I am about to say.

If you knowingly take delight in any creature, even for a
moment,[107] except insofar as it rouses you to devotion or instructs

104. Cf. *The Book of Margery Kempe*, I.83: "than had sche so many holy thowtys,
holy spechys, and dalyawns in hir sowle . . . that sche myth nevyr expressyn hem
wyth hir bodily tunge liche as sche felt hem." See also II.10, Kempe's universal bid-
ding prayer for all creatures.

105. *Marginal gloss:* "This is not just ordinary faith of which the text speaks, but
a certain formed and lively faith such as the Apostle defines: faith that hopes all
things, no doubt [cf. 1 Cor 13:7]. According to the Philosopher, it is vehement opinion. Concerning this, the apostle James advises us to ask in faith without hesitating
[Jas 1:6]. Without such faith, no one can ascend to the perfect love of God."

106. *Marginal gloss:* "According to the apostle Peter, 'cast all your cares on him,
for he cares for you.'" 1 Pet 5:7.

107. *Marginal gloss:* "That is, voluntarily, deliberately, and with full awareness.
Otherwise (as I said before), if someone takes delight in any creature unexpectedly
or out of weakness (even knowingly), he does not lose the fervor of love because of

you to delight in God, you will doubtless never have that special devotion that makes his dearest ones sing in the fire of charity. Almighty God, who is good, gives the sweetness of devotion to the unworthy by prevenient grace, alluring them this way in order to make them worthy,[108] insofar as any creature can be worthy of the Creator. No one is worthy, except in this way, if he knowingly takes delight in any creature—and so forth, as I have just said.[109]

O faith, faith, how great is your value! Perseverance, how noble you are! And you, my sluggish brother—you are seeking a remedy against the devil's temptations. Do not be cast down in despair—for I, your brother, was once tempted as you are, but never vanquished by it,[110] if I remember well. Thanks be to him who gave me this gift, to the Beloved, forever and ever—for I languish for love.

14. On the wonders performed through the name of Jesus

I have one remedy against all temptations. The Lord's name is a mighty tower; let the just man run to it and he will be exalted.[111] "In the name of Jesus I cast out demons; I speak in new tongues; I remove serpents, and if I drink any deadly thing, it does not harm me; I lay hands on the sick and they recover."[112] All these things I fulfill spiritually and—even more wonderfully—in myself. Although I sometimes extend charity to my neighbor, I am always a neighbor to myself. In the name of Jesus I find courage and constancy alike, both to live and to die, and thus I overcome every

---

it—unless this happens habitually and with gross negligence, or unless he has no qualms of conscience about it."

108. *Marginal gloss:* "That is, by rousing them with benefits."

109. *Marginal gloss:* "The holy David perceived this when he said, 'My soul refused to be comforted. I remembered God and took delight' [Ps 76:3-4]. But understand this carefully as stated above."

110. Cf. Heb 4:15.

111. Prov 18:10.

112. Mark 16:17-18.

deliberate temptation.[113] That is, I would sooner be physically killed by the devil than spiritually overcome by evil in any way. Go and do likewise[114] so that you can be free and, in consequence, sing with the angels—if you are among those so privileged.[115]

Venerating the name of Jesus, as I said above, is undoubtedly sufficient to defeat every enemy, for love is strong as death.[116] In the name of Jesus I cast out demons: when they visit me in my cell with many phantoms, spiritually and sometimes even visibly, they flee at this name without delay. In the name of Jesus I speak in new tongues, according to some who have heard or read the books I have written by God's grace. I say they are "new" because they are about the new life in Christ Jesus—glory to him forever![117] In the name of Jesus I remove serpents; my witnesses are those who have risen from sin.[118] (The serpents are demons.) In the name of Jesus, no deadly thing harms me in spirit when I hear of any evil, for I languish for love. (Evil is drunk in by hearing, just as a drink is by tasting.) I lay hands on the sick, for I arouse the lukewarm by word and example. Thanks be forever and ever to the Beloved, the giver of this gift. In the name of Jesus I do all these things, for I bear the name of Jesus in my mind while I do them with reverence and devotion. Thanks be to God forever, for I languish for love! So any evil that fights against me, whether it comes from the flesh, the world, or the devil, is conquered without delay when I bear the name of Jesus in my mind—and often on my lips as well. I do this firmly and faithfully because I languish for love.

113. *Marginal gloss:* "Because there is no great danger from temptations that sneak up unexpectedly or from the first motions of sin, which are not within human power. Yet (as he says) the faithful lover of Christ should sooner die than be deliberately overcome by any deadly temptation."

114. Luke 10:37.

115. *Marginal gloss:* "For there are few who acquire angelic song, nor is it given to anyone to experience this except by a great privilege of love."

116. Song 8:6.

117. Cf. Heb 13:21.

118. *Marginal gloss:* "Note the spiritual fulfillment of the Gospel."

15. Why God delays in giving perceptible love

In the seventh place, we must ask why a person sometimes languishes for love, that is, for a love that he wants to feel. Doubtless this happens because he does not perfectly direct his intention to the Beloved, or else the best time has not yet come. O how happy is the one who arrives at that point—but only if he has perfectly desired it. If only you have perfect desire, the Beloved cannot possibly leave you at that moment unless you leave him. It is amazing how he can hold himself back from embraces! But since he is supremely wise, he seizes his opportunity, so to speak. This is all for your good, for he has no need of your goods.[119] So let your heart take courage and wait for the Lord,[120] because your love for him cannot possibly be as great as his love for you.[121]

What then do you think is the cause of his delay, if not your imperfection? I dare say that in a sense, your imperfection is always the cause.[122] Otherwise, why should he wait—for his part, he is always ready—if not because of your imperfection?

You ask, "What imperfection can I have when I truly desire to be dissolved and be with him for his own sake, even if it were in hell?"[123]

I reply truthfully, "O man, these words are a stumbling block for you, unless they are interpreted in a very discreet, cautious way. If it were in hell, his glory would surely remain with him, for 'on those who dwell in the region of the shadow of death, a light has shone.'[124] So in this at least, you do not err."

---

119. Ps 15:2.
120. Ps 26:14.
121. Cf. *The Bedroom of the beloved Beloved*, chap. 26.
122. *Marginal gloss:* "That is, either because you have not yet prepared yourself or because you have acted negligently, or because you could not endure the fervor of love, or perhaps if you had perceptible love, you would become proud."
123. Desiring to be with God "even in hell" is a common topos in mystics. Methley shows himself skeptical, perhaps because "hell" is by definition the place where God is absent.
124. Isa 9:2; Matt 4:16.

"Why, O why do you say that I err?"

"Again, you are a stumbling block to yourself. How? Listen and I will explain two ways that you err and become a stumbling block. You desire to be dissolved; this is the first error.[125] (You are the one who asked me to explain how you err; it wasn't my idea!) There is a second error as well. In the first, it seems that you want your own will to be done. In the second, your impatience made you blind and erring, so you lied. Amend these two evils in your whole way of life! If you ask whose fault it is, God is the one waiting for you, not you for him."

True, a wish to be dissolved because of languishing love belongs to the highest perfection. Yet one who is governed by reason errs if he does not commit the whole affair to God.[126] And for a spiritual man to incur any error or falsehood through impetuosity is a vice, a great imperfection.

Bear these things in mind, brothers, so you can understand how the Beloved delays until he has an opportunity—even though he is almighty. If you have long desired a perceptible devotion, see that you are not culpable in either of these ways. For I suppose no subtler temptation attacks the spiritual man than what I have written. Be forewarned against these faults, therefore, and never stop loving. But say with heart and voice both day and night, "O Jesus, Jesus! I languish for love."

125. *Marginal gloss:* "I don't see what the author means here, unless it is that no one should desire to be dissolved and be with Christ [Phil 1:23] if he does not also entrust his whole self to God. Otherwise he would be following his own comfort and his own will, for there is no one who does not wish to be blessed. Again, a spiritual person should beware of doing or saying anything in impetuosity or impatience. Nor should he be stubborn or pertinacious in his opinion, for charity is patient and kind." 1 Cor 13:4.

126. *Marginal gloss:* "He says this because in the rapture of contemplation (which is above reason), a person is not bound to propose such reasons."

16. How to begin the purest contemplation

Here is an eighth way to understand love's languor. A person who does feel perceptible love is punished above all because he does not yet see the Beloved.[127]

"O languishing one! What will you give me to show him to you?"

"After I renounced the whole world, I had nothing."

"O wealthy pauper! The one for whom you gave it all up can repay you a hundredfold.[128] Be faithful to him, for I tell you truly that he languishes for your love. So if you want to see him, come with me and I will show him to you. For I myself have seen him, and I know that he wants you to see him too. This is the way that I walked."[129]

When devotion awakens your longing to see the Beloved, prepare a suitable place where you can make a habit of sitting in pure contemplation. In this exalted mood, direct your mind above, hoping to see him whom you love above all. When you have arranged a suitable time and place, you should have a moderately soft seat. Insofar as you can, sit in private to avoid the gaze of scoffers. Then close your eyes or, if you wish, lower your hood so that you will see no created things, but raise your mind above. Set the image of the cross before your eyes after saying, "Come holy Spirit,"[130] and "in the name of the Father and of the Son and of the Holy Spirit, Amen."

Use this preparatory prayer, or a better prayer if you know one, unless you receive some heavenly inspiration in pure affection:[131]

---

127. The following passage makes best sense if read as a short dialogue between master and disciple.

128. Matt 19:29. Cf. *The Refectory of Salvation*, chap. 1.

129. *Marginal gloss:* "Preparation for contemplation."

130. Cf. the sequence for Pentecost, *Veni sancte Spiritus*.

131. *Marginal gloss:* "For mental and affective prayer is purer and more efficacious if God inspires it."

"O my almighty God, three and one, good and eternal, living and true:[132] Whatever exists is good because of you, and this I offer you, for I languish for love for your sake, now and forever. Receive me, for you are good forever and ever. Amen."

Later I can explain more suitably how you should proceed, as the Lord wills. Sit for fifteen minutes at dawn, fifteen minutes after noon, and the same after midnight. But after Vespers or supper, you can double this time as I do myself to half an hour. (Thanks to the Beloved for endless ages!) When you rise after the time is over, say this prayer if you wish, or a better prayer if you know one:[133] "O sweetest Beloved, long have I awaited you and I truly long to see you, if it be your will. But while you delay, intensify my desire lest I fall away, for I languish for love. As you wish and as you can, have mercy on us, for you are supremely good and you can do all things. To you be praise, to you be glory, to you be thanksgiving forever and ever. Saint Mary and the whole court of heaven, pray for us. Amen. For I truly languish for love."

17. On the form of ascent by unknowing in contemplation[134]

Now I must set down the form of ascent by unknowing in the purest contemplation, as I said above: "later I can explain how you should proceed." This is the most important point: anyone who languishes for love, and longs in some way to see the One on whom angels desire to gaze,[135] must purify the eyes.[136] Can a person whose eyes rove to the ends of the earth[137] expect to see

---

132. *Marginal gloss:* "Prayer." Cf. the Canon of the Mass: *reddunt vota sua eterno Deo vivo et vero*.

133. *Marginal gloss:* "Prayer."

134. Methley writes here in the apophatic tradition of Dionysius the Areopagite (*De mystica theologia*) and *The Cloud of Unknowing*, which he translated into Latin.

135. 1 Pet 1:12.

136. *Marginal gloss:* "For God cannot be contemplated with troubled eyes, just as the physical eye cannot see clearly when it is dimmed by smoke or dust."

137. Cf. Job 28:24.

the Beloved in a corner of the choir or the church? So first amend what is greater; then rise to the lesser. If you are roused by devotion to attain the vision of God, pay attention now—for I am speaking to you and those like you. You cannot possibly be cheated of your desire if you persevere in this good.

Once again, no one is fit for the purest contemplation unless he first languishes for love in devotion.[138] While you languish, you will behave like a sick person.[139] At other times you will sit quite properly, awakening or awaiting the glory of contemplation by making a special effort in devotion.[140] But sick people, when they are in very bad shape, lay aside or completely forget everything else in the violent fit of their illness—whether the fear of pain or the love of glory, whether they are carnal lovers or spiritual ones. As long as they languish for love, only what they languish for remains fixed in their minds.

So it will be for you. Yet in some ways, take note, you will do the opposite. While you are languishing, you cannot actually feel your sickness, for it can banish all that is painful. Because of the violence of love, people who are languishing forget everything around them, whether in themselves or another. Just as those who languish with a physical illness sometimes go out of their minds in ecstasy,[141] you ought to do this spiritually in your small degree.[142] But you will also do the exact opposite: you will utterly cast out fear because, during your rapture, you can feel nothing

---

138. *Marginal gloss:* "Because the fervor of love is the highway to pure contemplation."

139. *Marginal gloss:* "For just as a sick person desires nothing so much as health, one who languishes in love desires nothing but the Beloved, for whose love he is fainting in all his limbs, so he is unable to think about anything else."

140. *per industriam contemplacionis gloriam in devocione precipuam.* As the context makes clear, the "effort" pertains to devotion, not contemplation.

141. *excessum incurrunt mentis.* In mystical writing, *excessus mentis* is a technical term for ecstasy. But it can also denote a temporary state of madness due to illness or some physical cause.

142. *Marginal gloss:* "But this happens by God's gift."

but joy.[143] Even when you remember pain, you will not fear it because you are overwhelmed by joy. In this way too, you will rise by unknowing[144] and utterly forget all that is painful.[145] Note that I said *utterly*. In the third place, this is the most miraculous thing of all: You will do the opposite of the sick person because you will utterly forget the glory of heaven. Here again, note that I said *utterly*.[146] Otherwise you could not experience ecstasy, where the glory of contemplation resides.

Perhaps you will say, "these things are against reason! And not only that, but I cannot possibly achieve them!" I concede both points. Indeed, if these things were rational, perhaps even pagans could achieve them. Again, if they were possible for anyone who wished, all Christians would boast of their knowledge in this matter.[147] But neither is the case. Contemplation is above reason because, just as no one can say what God is, God cannot be seen by any effort in prayer.[148] Yet, for the great benefit of humankind, God reserved this wisdom for himself so that everyone who loves (even the simplest person) may presume to ask the Beloved for something he does not have, and indeed cannot have, by himself. And God clearly shows how near he is to those who love him when he says, "Before you call upon me, I will say 'here I am.' "[149]

---

143. *Marginal gloss:* "Because love banishes fear." 1 John 4:18.

144. *Ignote. Marginal gloss:* "He says *by unknowing* because reason has no use in that ecstatic contemplation, and according to the criteria of reason, a person does not know what he is doing then."

145. *Marginal gloss:* "For in that ecstasy in God, the soul is passive rather than active. I say 'passive' not because it experiences any pain or sorrow, but only the working of God."

146. *Marginal gloss:* "For the soul does not remember any being then (that is, in that ecstasy) except God alone, who remains in the cloud and dwells in unapproachable light." 1 Tim 6:16.

147. *Marginal gloss:* "Rather, it is a gift of God lest anyone should boast." Eph 2:9.

148. *per oracionis industriam.* Richard of St. Victor similarly uses *industria* to refer to effort in prayer. Cf. his *Benjamin Minor*, chap. 74, "On that kind of contemplation that is above reason."

149. Cf. Isa 65:24.

I will briefly review these points. You must utterly forget everything, both creation and the Creator, in order to rise by unknowing. Do you see what I have said? In this single word *unknowing*, I have summed up the whole matter. If you know anything, your knowledge is false[150]—not according to revelation,[151] but as far as the purest contemplation goes. If you know nothing, but were ravished unknowingly into the light, without mediation—knowing nothing before, during, or after your ecstasy—this, I say, is the true work of your contemplation.[152] For afterward, when the man of God deliberates with himself a while later—I no longer say "without mediation" as before, but with mediation[153]—then he first understands that he was ravished into the supremely marvelous light. O sweet is the light, and delectable to the eyes to behold the sun! For I languish for love.

18. On a temptation by the devil in the practice of contemplation

I sigh for a sight of the sempiternal sun, yet I am dragged down in delights by the devil's deception so that, tested by temptation

---

150. *Marginal gloss:* "Here he explains what it means to rise by unknowing."

151. *Marginal gloss:* "For revelation can indeed be attained by the use of reason, while the use of the other senses also remains."

152. *Marginal gloss:* "For God is found in the cloud of unknowing. Contemplation therefore is true and pure when someone is suddenly ravished above himself into that marvelous and spiritual light that is God, of which it is said, 'He was the true light,' etc. [John 1:9]. He also says that the intellectual power does not enter into that rapture, but remains outside, whereas affection is always allowed to enter. Therefore the Apostle confesses this spiritual unknowing: 'Whether in the body or out of the body I do not know, God knows,' etc." [2 Cor 12:2]. Cf. Hugh of St. Victor: "He is loved more fully than he is understood, and love enters and draws near where knowledge remains outside." *Commentary on the* Celestial Hierarchy *of Dionysius the Areopagite*, book 6.

153. A play on words. Methley contrasts Latin *mediate* with *immediate* (both "immediately" and "without mediation by creatures"). *Marginal gloss:* "He says *mediate*, that is, a while later. For a person cannot immediately and at once discern how, with full deliberation."

or terrified by tribulation, I might turn back from the throne of the Trinity.[154] For truly, truly, I languish for love! You who made me, have mercy on me and manifest yourself to me, for I languish for love! I despise the deceits of the devil, for I languish for love. Last night, in the third hour after midnight on the feast of the most blessed Saints Sixtus and Agapetus[155] in the year 1484, the thirty-third year of my life (if I am correct), while I was sitting to practice contemplation, the devil made himself suddenly, unexpectedly present, testing me by this means. But thanks to the Beloved, he lost the battle and finally sat in darkness (as is fitting) at my feet— or (I will speak more plainly) on my right foot. He cried out horribly and wondrously, but did not notably frighten me after the first movement. Later, having thought about this, I was sitting in contemplation as before and did not get up because of him, all his wiles notwithstanding. So you too, man, should know that such contemplation, which makes our enemy the devil pine away like this, is worthier and better than all the voluntary exercises of the spiritual life. This could be proven by other authorities. But I will go on to other things, for I languish for love.

19. On the martyrdom of having two contrary feelings at the same time[156]

In the ninth place, a person can languish for love because he voluntarily unites his will (as he should) with the will of the Beloved. This is martyrdom for him because of his surpassing languor. I suppose no mortal can understand, if he has not experienced it, how these two feelings actually, perceptibly coexist in a single

---

154. Methley imitates the alliterative style of Richard Rolle's *Melos amoris*.

155. August 6. The Carthusians did not observe the feast of the Transfiguration on this date.

156. *De duobus quodammodo contrariis in affeccione cum martirio.* This chapter is translated loosely because its impetuous, elliptical style leaves much to the reader's intuition. The text seems to be corrupt at several points.

person. On the one hand, he wills what the Beloved wills, that is, that he should remain in the flesh. On the other, with affection and tears, he wishes to be dissolved and be with Christ.[157] Someone might easily object that he has these two feelings at different times. But I say that I have experienced this contradiction (thanks to the Beloved), and that is why I speak of it. What I say now is the truth if I am truthful.

If you understand what an instant is, you speak truly, for an instant cannot be divided,[158] nor can reason distinguish two thoughts in one instant. I know you can understand the experience I have described as taking place at two different times. Yet all at once, as we commonly say—in a single brief prayer, perhaps two instants long—a person can feel both sentiments I spoke of. To speak more plainly, the grace of the Beloved no doubt works this wonder in him. If you should think one of these feelings is rational and the other emotional, that would not be hard to understand.[159] But the marvel, as I have said, is that both are experienced emotionally.[160] I know by experience (thanks be to God forever!) that this is absolutely true.

Justly, then, the man of God suffers martyrdom and languishes profoundly. Living is death to him, for he loves the Beloved so

157. Speaking from experience, Methley analyzes the dilemma expressed by Saint Paul in Phil 1:23. One clause of this sentence, omitted in the text, is supplied by Hand B at the foot of the page.

158. *Marginal gloss:* "An instant is a unit of time so brief that it cannot be divided." Cf. *The Cloud of Unknowing*, where it is explained that an instant or "atom" of time is just long enough for a single act of will (chap. 4) or a single prayer of one syllable (chap. 7).

159. *Marginal gloss:* "For reason can dictate, even though affection may not consent." Methley's *affectio* means both "affection" and emotion or feeling in a broader sense.

160. *Marginal gloss:* "Yet both can indeed happen [at once], for affection is very often tearful and easily deflected to either side, so that it can desire a thing that in some way displeases it. Thus the apostle Paul cried out, emotionally torn in two directions, saying, 'I am compelled on both sides, and which I shall choose I do not know, having a desire to be dissolved,' etc." Phil 1:23.

ardently that he would wish to die if the Beloved were to allow it.[161] Yet to die without merit, without honor to the Beloved, would be death to him no less than to remain in the flesh. Therefore he is a glorious confessor of the Lord because he suffers martyrdom either way, living or dying.[162] So he can say,[163] without needing the example of all the martyrs and confessors in their degrees,[164] "I languish for love."

20. On four wonders concerning the author of this book; on his ennui; and on the ennui of lovers of the world

In the tenth place, we must explain how someone languishes for love when he finds it tiresome to be alive on earth for even a moment. Who could believe there is anyone superior to the person described in the previous chapter? Yet the love of Christ compels me to speak,[165] for beyond the least doubt, I do know someone superior to him, whom I will now describe. Let my enemies scoff or be silent, for (thanks be to God) if such people exist, I myself am one.

As I am very often ravished in contemplation, I know by revelation what the Beloved wills, and I have acquired grace to seek grace and, through that grace, to accomplish his will. It is through grace that I hold these three desires in mind:[166] the will to be dissolved, the will to live, and the will to be presented to the Beloved in a moment because of ennui. Greater than all of these is this: I would rather be thrust beneath Lucifer in hell for as long as I am going to live on earth than be kept back from the Beloved for one

---

161. *Marginal gloss:* "He desires to die so that from now on, he may be with Christ. He also refuses to die so that he may be conformed to the will of God—and both are emotional responses [*utrumque . . . in affeccione*], as stated above."

162. A confessor is a saint who suffers persecution for the faith, but not to the point of death.

163. *Marginal gloss:* "According to the will of the Beloved, to which he is united."

164. *sine exemplo omnium predictorum in gradibus suis.* The text is obscure.

165. Cf. 2 Cor 5:14.

166. *Marginal gloss:* "Because of the will's conformity to God."

moment after death, in purgatory or even in Paradise. (Let's not even mention hell after death!) The most vehement love compels me to confess this. Ordinarily, divine mercy treats us very well if we are received into Paradise as soon as we die.

O ennui, how inscrutable you are to those who have no knowledge of you! Ennui, holy ennui! How different you are from the ennui that many people experience during the Divine Office or other good works. Those who love this world constantly suffer from ennui, even if they deny it,[167] when they read or sing about your love, good Jesus, or work or write. How great our love ought to be when the God whom we love is so near! It is said of him, "he is near to those who return to their hearts."[168] For he is found in the heart, even if every lover of this world denies it. As long as you love the world and follow the judgment of reason, you will be afraid to die for love of the Beloved.[169] O Jesus Christ, my lover, thanks be to you for endless ages, for I languish for love!

21. On the betrothal between God and the soul. On the first place in purgatory, with the analogy of a sick person and his recovery

In the eleventh place, I speak of one who languishes for love because he fears being held back from the Beloved after death. He can scarcely bear any delay even in Paradise, for he is satisfied with no good less than God as he is seen in the empyrean heaven.[170] Nor does he believe he can be satisfied—for he languishes vehemently for love.

---

167. *Marginal gloss:* "Because nothing is so laborious to lovers of this world as to put their labor aside, that is, to be occupied with spiritual things." An allusion to Rolle's *Contra amatores mundi* (*Against Lovers of the World*).

168. Ps 84:9.

169. *Marginal gloss:* "For to desire this out of pure affection is a gift of God."

170. *Marginal gloss:* "For the soul is not satisfied except with the highest good." The empyrean, or heaven of fire, is the highest heaven, in which God is most clearly seen.

Any man who is beloved yearns to marry the bride he has desired for many years. As his wedding day approaches, he adorns himself honorably in beautiful, elegant clothes. Nothing (God forbid!) should offend his bride, whom he loves most chastely as his fiancée. But suppose that he falls gravely ill with some unforeseen, unexpected sickness. If he escapes death, he must first recover from his illness enough to at least sit up in bed. Once he has fully regained his strength, he strives to fulfill the desire that he had before. So, to return to our point, the man who is beloved of Eternal Wisdom, or rather the supreme Trinity, yearns to be joined with her in marriage after he dies.[171] Or conversely, let him be the bride; the bridegroom is God, who takes the soul as his bride.[172] In either case, he passionately yearns to fly up to heaven at once. And indeed he will—if guilt does not stand in his way. Then he will have what he has long desired, to enjoy without end.

Glory to you, O Christ! You have unlocked heaven for us after we die, so that we need not pass like the ancients into the limbo of the fathers.[173] How many people would be glad to go straight to heaven when they die—yet they do not wish to abstain from sin here on earth.[174] But let us return to our purpose. If a person is not worthy to go straight to heaven after death, he will doubtless be purified in purgatory, if he is to be saved, or else he will be made worthy in Paradise to enter the empyrean heaven.[175] So if

171. *Marginal gloss:* "The devout soul, who is the bride of God, yearns to be joined to her beloved Bridegroom after death, like an earthly bridegroom after recovering from sickness. For the holy soul recovers from sickness when she is delivered by death, so that she can fly to the Bridegroom."

172. Methley alludes to Henry Suso's *Horologium Sapientiae* (*The Clock of Wisdom*), in which Christ appears as the Bridegroom of the soul but also as the feminine Eternal Wisdom, whom the seeker desires as a bride.

173. At the harrowing of hell, between his death and his resurrection, Christ visited hell and "preached to the spirits in prison" (1 Pet 3:19), delivering the righteous souls of the Old Testament from limbo.

174. *Marginal gloss:* "Always take note."

175. *Marginal gloss:* "For there is a purgatory of desire, where it is necessary for everyone who is imperfect in the love of God to be purified even after the purgatory of pain, before entering the empyrean heaven."

he is in purgatory,[176] to follow our analogy, he is like that sick man before his wedding, and he has to be cured.[177] This is because he did not first adorn himself in beauty and glory, as he should have, to keep from offending the chaste soul of the bride whom he loves. Just as doctors comfort sick people with sweeter, better foods than the usual kind in order to cure them, those who lie in the fire of purgatory are helped by their friends with Masses, alms, and other good works.

This is the first place in purgatory. Keep me out of it, O God, for I languish for love!

22. On the second place in purgatory, with the analogy of a convalescent; and on small sins

The second place could be called a kind of Paradise, yet in a way it is purgatorial,[178] for the soul is purged there until it is made worthy in its way of heaven. Resurrected like a patient healed from sickness, the soul regains its strength there until it can walk and finally attend its wedding.[179] But if I'm not mistaken, it is fed there with the most delicious and efficacious foods, namely contemplations of the heavenly court, much more luminous than it could ever enjoy in the world. In this way it is made fit for heaven. I am not speaking to you alone, you lovers of this world, but also to you lovers of God—religious men, hermits and cenobites. You may avoid great sins, yet you take little account of the smallest ones. Remember what is written: "I have given you a day instead

176. *Marginal gloss:* "That is, the purgatory of pain."

177. *Marginal gloss:* "That is, by purification. For if the soul had first been truly, perfectly adorned with the love of God and other virtues, doubtless it would not have come to that place."

178. *Marginal gloss,* apparently by Methley himself: "As I have explained above."

179. In otherworld visions, including Dante's *Commedia,* the earthly Paradise is an intermediate resting place between purgatory and heaven. In the *Revelation of Purgatory* to the anchoress of Winchester (1422), the revenant (a nun) undergoes fierce purgatorial torments before reaching the earthly Paradise, where she is prepared for her marriage to Christ.

of a year."[180] How greatly the people in that place desire to see God, and how long it seems to linger there for a year, instead of the one day in this world when we could voluntarily do penance! Desire then will be at its zenith, and the time will seem exceedingly long. Deliver me from these things, O God, for I languish for love.

23. On the third place in purgatory and its analogy. On the smallest thought, and on the betrothal of the bride

The third place comes after the soul has recovered its strength, when there remains only the betrothal or the desire, according to the analogy I proposed above. O Jesus, Jesus! O Jesus! I would rather endure every pain there is, if it were your will (and if it were possible), than fall into the anguish of standing at that door forever—knocking,[181] seeking entrance, and being put off until the morrow. When I say that I cannot bear a single moment of delay, I speak according to the deliberate affection of desire.

O what a Paradise, what a marvelous purgatory—to live in delight, in a way, and yet to be pierced with the sword of longing for the Beloved![182] Who could imagine how deeply those souls repent of the least evil thought, when they could in a single day have redeemed themselves? So do your penance now, beloved, whoever you are, if you desire this bride or this friend. For Scripture says truly, "Nothing defiled enters into her" (Wis 7).[183] Nothing, I say, nothing at all! O my God, spare me if possible so I need not come to that place—or if I cannot escape it, deign to shorten

180. *Marginal gloss:* "Because one day of true penance in this world is equivalent to a whole year in purgatory after death." The quotation is not biblical, but cf. Ps 89:4 and 2 Pet 3:8.

181. Cf. Rev 3:20.

182. *Marginal gloss:* "This is because in that place, they do not yet have a perfect vision of God."

183. Wis 7:25.

the time. For what reason concedes, affection denies,[184] because I languish for love.

24. On languor caused by the struggle between flesh and spirit. Who will enter glory after death without delay

Finally, in the twelfth place, a person languishes for love because the greatest struggle pits the spirit against the flesh.[185] The spirit yearns to depart continually and at once, while the flesh resists. Now, my dearest ones, my heart is troubled within me! Yet God, who gave me the gift of yearning to be dissolved, has also shown me his will and united my will to himself, as it ought to be. Thanks to him forever and ever! Between flesh and spirit, that is, between body and soul, I experience the greatest struggle within myself. Quite often, it seems to me, my soul is at the very point of departing, and I open my mouth as if to breathe forth my spirit. Yet this wretched flesh (woe is me that I do not yet die!)—this wretched flesh constrains my spirit so that I cannot send it forth.[186] I marvel how I can endure this. But since nothing God wills is impossible for him,[187] I cannot die until he wills it. Therefore I languish so much for love—so very much! That is why I pray the Beloved that I may not be kept back from him after I die. But let these pains I suffer, which are the pains of a chaste desire, be my purgatory—for I languish for love! I truly know that if I pass away because of this exceedingly great, languishing love, I will enter into glory and not into punishment.[188]

You who created me, have mercy on me and on all Christian people. My orthodox and catholic brothers, correct this work if

---

184. *Marginal gloss:* "Because impatient love believes that all things yield to it."
185. Gal 5:17.
186. *Marginal gloss:* "For the body that is corrupted vexes the soul." Wis 9:15.
187. Matt 19:26; Luke 1:37.
188. *Marginal gloss:* "He speaks from the instinct of affection, for otherwise (as it is written) a person does not know whether he deserves love or hatred." Eccl 9:1.

there is need, and if it pleases you, copy it. Praise God with me forever, I beg you, for I languish for love.

Here ends the book called *The School of Languishing Love*.

A Devout Prayer on the Name of Jesus and on the Five Wounds[1]

O Jesus, good ruler of morals
And savior of the ages,
Song of those who deserve you:
May the holy wound of your right hand
End the lament of our hearts
After the way of lovers.

Eternal, exalted King
And most delicious bread,
Food of those who enjoy you:
May the wound of your left hand
Bless us, lest the infernal Vulcan
Burn the hearts of believers.

Hail Jesus, hail Jesus,
Music to the ear, honey in the mouth,
Health of those who love you:
May the broad wound of your right foot
Purge our guilt away,
Salvation of the weak and sick.

Burn our loins, breath of holy fire,
Our helper and advocate,

---

1. Devotion to the Name of Jesus and his Five Wounds was widespread in Methley's day. See R. W. Pfaff, *New Liturgical Feasts in Later Medieval England* (Oxford: Oxford University Press, 1970), 62–91. The author of this poem is unknown, though it could be Methley himself. Its rhyme scheme is AABCCB.

Life of those who behold you:
May the open wound of your left foot
Expose the hidden wound of our hearts
In the way of confessors.

Hail Jesus, good Jesus,
In the union of love,
Holiness of those who live in you:
May the wound of your pierced heart
Heal the wounds of the desperate
And the hearts of those who sing.

Verse: O Jesus, may your name and your five wounds
Response: Save us from every slaughter.

Let us pray.

O God, almighty Father, who through your only-begotten Son Jesus Christ and through his cross and passion resolved to save the world; grant, we beseech, that through the invocation of his name and the veneration of his wounds, we may deserve pardon and grace in the present and happily attain to glory unknown in the future, through the same Jesus Christ our Lord.

The Bedroom of the beloved Beloved

Here is the angelic greeting to begin a book called *The Bedroom of the beloved Beloved*. "Hail Mary, full of grace, the Lord is with you. Blessed are you among women and blessed is the fruit of your womb, Jesus. Amen."[1] And blessed be your most holy mother Anne, of whom your immaculate, virginal flesh was born.[2] Amen.

Here begins the prologue to the aforesaid book, *The Bedroom of the beloved Beloved*.[3]

In the past, gracious Creator, you gave me the ability to write about you while I was awake. But now, as best I can, I want to disclose the celestial glory I experience while I am miraculously awake in sleep,[4] because I know that you want this too. For you languish for my love and I for yours[5]—but this languor causes

---

1. The *Ave Maria* derives from Luke 1:28 and 1:42.

2. An allusion to the Immaculate Conception, still a debated doctrine at this time.

3. The phrase *dilectus dilectus* (Ps 67:13), or "beloved beloved," is a superlative form equivalent to *dilectissimus*. In the title it can also mean "one beloved by the Beloved," i.e., Christ.

4. Song 5:2, "I sleep and my heart is awake," a key refrain. *Ego dormio (I Sleep)* is a work by Richard Rolle.

5. Song 2:5. "Languishing for love" is the second refrain and key concept of the work.

me to sleep, and you as well. I have no doubt that as the proverb goes, in both of us this sleep is a sign of health, not sickness.

Because we are speaking to one another here, I believe that *The Bedroom of the beloved Beloved* is an apt title for this little book. O my Beloved, I beg you, in this bedroom let there be a single bed for us both—and then I have no doubt that our sleep will be sweet! Indeed, this is marvelous: I am healthy because I sleep, yet I also languish because I sleep. Further, this is yet more marvelous: I am awake and asleep at the same time, and at once healthy and languishing. In the following pages I will explain all this. But here I will not fail to add that I have such a great hope of love in the glorious Virgin Mary, your mother and mine, that I long for her honor in all things. That is why I began with the angelic greeting, for I know that she will make haste to help me. *Here ends the prologue.*

Here begins the book called *The Bedroom of the beloved Beloved.*

1. On the mode of speech in the aforesaid bedroom

"I sleep and my heart is awake." At the very beginning, the literal sense proves to be impossible, so we must turn our pen to a spiritual understanding. Because it is the master who is supposed to teach, not the student, I beg you to teach me—and through me, teach others. Truly I know your will: in this book you want me to write with you in a new mode of speaking, a most truthful mode. Sometimes this will be through inspiration, though differently than before. At other times it will be in dialogue, as in the many books I have already written through you.[6] But here you speak to me through your very self, without intermediary, in an ordinary style of speech. Yet at times you also want to teach me through inspiration without supplying a name.

---

6. A reference to earlier, lost works.

The Lord says to me, "In this volume of yours, write all the words I speak to you in *The Bedroom of the beloved Beloved*.[7] For you are beloved to me, well beloved; and I am beloved to you, incomparably beloved."

"I sleep, Lord, but you alone know how."

"As for you, teach others so that they too can learn to sleep, once they have been provided with this bedroom and you have been laid in the grave."

"Lord, this is the only thing I desire in this world, and therefore I languish for love. But I have not yet explained how it is that I sleep."

2. *How one must sleep*

It seems wondrous that a mortal could sleep while he is awake and be awake while he is sleeping. I know what sleep is and what waking is, so it is with great wonder that I see them coexist at the same time in the same way.

The Lord says to me, "Teach them how one must ascend step by step to learn to sleep in the bedroom of the beloved Beloved."

Step by step, my brothers, is how one must ascend to this bedroom. So whoever wants to sleep should ascend the first step by fully believing that those who love God purely, for his own sake, cannot lack any useful thing either here or in the future life. In this way he will have peace from external anxieties so he can sleep. Second, he should fully believe that as long as he retains the use of the five senses, he must absolutely never omit anything to which he is bound by obedience—though some things can be delayed for awhile, or changed for the better, and afterward be done again as they were before. Third, let him know that all things have their time.[8] So in spiritual matters, two things should never be done at once because, without special grace, they cannot both

7. Cf. Jer 30:2 and 36:2.
8. Eccl 3:1.

be done well. In this way he will have peace from the hubbub of domestic concerns.

Fourth, he should firmly understand that he must not set any condition for himself, whether in affairs of the will,[9] the spirit, or the body, where he is ignorant. Rather, let him offer his whole self to God and, when the time comes, experience will infallibly teach him whether he has attained a knowledge of truth and falsehood. Fifth, anyone who wishes to sleep and be awake at once should not set a definite time, but wait for you at all times, always ready. Then when you come, he will not miss you out of reliance on old habits.

See, now I have spoken.

3. How great is the joy of this wakefulness

The Lord says to me, "Tell them how great is the joy of this wakefulness in which you glory so much."

Truly I begin to be foolish, for I cannot speak unless you, God, put a word in the mouth of my heart—the word I must write to them. This joy is so great that no mortal creature can tell of it, nor can anyone presume to comprehend it in itself. Yet I am allowed to proclaim something of it to others insofar as you bid me tell them. Think how great a difference there is between a dying man in his last agony and a flourishing youth who revels in his strength. Know then that there is a difference just as great—or incomparably greater—between the highest pleasure one can enjoy among creatures in sin and the infinite pleasure to be enjoyed in God for his own sake.

4. That the love of God deserves veneration

But let no one suppose from this analogy that he could imagine or describe even the least joy of truly divine love. For just as God

9. Reading *voluntariis* for MS *voluptariis*.

is ineffable, his love in a true lover cannot be expressed. Such a lover is one who loves God for his own sake and would not sin even if he were allowed to do so with impunity. Let no one flatter himself that he is a true lover unless he senses that condition in his own heart in a perceptible way—just as perceptibly as if he felt his finger burnt in the fire.[10] Such perceptible feelings[11] are very common in supremely perfect men, as I have said. I will say it again: in supremely perfect men, for many may seem perfect both to themselves and to others, yet not to God. Search me, O God, and know my heart,[12] for I languish for love. If I say this in order to be praised and not for your own sake, let me be deprived of you and the heavenly crown.

5. On the intensity of divine love

Such a person must sleep in this novel way, for he is so perfect that every creature is burdensome to him—every creature in heaven or on earth. This is not because he despises any creature; rather, he is so afflicted by desire for the Creator that no creature can comfort him. Let me clarify this with an analogy. When a person has been searching for someone he loves very much and is so grief-stricken that he seems to have lost his mind, suppose he sees someone who resembles his beloved. But when he comes closer, he realizes that this is not the one he is seeking. Then he is stung, or rather pierced through the heart, by a fresh sting. It is the same in this case, for whenever it occurs to me that I could be consoled by any creature, my pain is renewed and I nearly faint. So I can well say, "I sleep and my heart is awake."

10. Cf. Richard Rolle, *Incendium Amoris*, Prologue.
11. *Affectus sensibiles*. For Methley, love is a disposition of the will, yet in its perfect state it is experienced in both the emotions and the senses.
12. Ps 138:23.

6. On the three virtues of sleep

The first virtue of this sleep is to have no anxiety. To obtain this virtue, solitude helps a great deal—if one truly dwells alone in spirit, not just in body. The second virtue is to avoid distraction. To preserve that virtue, it is most helpful to guard the eyes from both licit and illicit things, as far as it is permitted and possible. The third virtue is that a solitary should be ready to live and die for the love of Christ. So he will not grumble, nor can he be overcome by any temptation. For it is written, "Glory to God in the highest," and in consequence it is said, "and on earth peace." That peace is not for lovers of this world, but "for people of good will."[13] Therefore, anyone whose character is of this kind can safely say, without flattering himself or others, "I sleep and my heart is awake."

7. On the excellence of true obedience

But there is one virtue that surpasses all others and far excels them, because it alone makes a man perfect. Some might say it is charity—but I say it is true obedience.[14] This virtue is practiced in community among regular monks and in singularity between God and his highest anchorite.[15] So I will explain, as I have learned from experience, why the solitary should be called a king above all mortals and a mortal who has no peer in true obedience. He is indeed subject to the sole king of the ages, the immortal and invisible God, to whom be honor and glory forever and ever.[16] That is why the humble Pope Gregory called himself "the servant of the servants of God."[17] Someone who is given responsibility

13. Luke 2:14; the liturgical *Gloria*.

14. A view shared by Methley's fellow Carthusian, John Norton: *Musica monachorum*, cap. 5, pars 2.

15. *anacoritam summum*, a hermit.

16. 1 Tim 1:17.

17. The papal title *servus servorum Dei*, first adopted by Gregory I.

for another is free from anxiety, in a way, and can dedicate himself to devotion. He is like a king who has entrusted everything that concerns him to his officials, so he has leisure for the pursuits he enjoys the most.

Let us see then who is a slave and who a master. Would you not call someone who has toil and anxiety a slave, and the other a master? One who is truly obedient has nothing to be anxious about. If an office is entrusted to him out of obedience, this does not happen by his own will. Rather, it is the will of the prelate who appoints him, or at any rate the will of God, so he has no anxiety when he exercises his office. Whether someone is a regular monk or a solitary, such as an anchorite or a recluse, only true obedience frees him from anxiety. If some difficulty arises, let him seek the judgment of his superior. In this way he may truthfully, not fallaciously, say, "I sleep and my heart is awake."

8. That the lover of God is asleep and awake at the same time

A sleeper naturally does not think about the love of the world as waking people do. So a person who takes such delight in the love of God that he forgets the love of the world is awake in the love of God, asleep to the love of the world. What does it mean to be asleep to the love of the world? To take no more pleasure in it than if he were sleeping. Conversely, a person who takes such delight in the love of the world that he forgets the love of God is asleep to the love of God, awake in the love of the world. What does it mean to be asleep to the love of God? To take no more pleasure in it than if he were sleeping.

A person who sleeps in one respect is awake in the other. That is, one who is asleep to the love of God is awake in the love of the world; one who is awake in the love of God is asleep to the love of the world. Sleeping means taking no pleasure; being awake means taking pleasure. What I have just said makes it clear that what I wrote in the prologue is true, surprising though it is. Namely, the lover of God is asleep and awake at one and the same time.

9. *That health and sickness occur at the same time in a person*

But I have not yet explained how a person can be healthy and sick at the same time, for this health or well-being cannot be separated from sickness.[18] A man of God is sometimes healthy in body, sometimes in spirit. But if this sickness is in the spirit, it heals the spirit, and commonly speaking, it even relieves the body from sickness for a time. But listen now to something even more to the point: this sickness proceeds from health. For if a person is healthy in spirit and free from vices, according to his capacity and way of life—that is, if he is the beloved beloved (I mean if he is specially chosen above many others)—he begins to languish. The healthier he is, the sicker he becomes. And if at last, as he languishes, he is perfectly ravished above himself, then he has what he desires: the kiss of love, which is the greatest happiness on earth. By this he is so fully healed that, if he were to depart this world in such a state, he would never feel the pains of purgatory, but enter at once into joy. It is clear from what I have said, therefore, that health and sickness occur together.

10. *How some people excuse themselves from the love of God*

Let no one think I could tell how great is the joy of this health, or how great the distress of this sickness—if indeed it can be called distress, rather than delight.[19] Yet, because I know it is God's will to offer at least a mouthful of this drink to those who desire it, I will pour out a tiny bit for the thirsty—one drop of the sea, so to speak. But first, readers, I want you all to know that I am not seeking my own glory, as God is my witness. Rather, I seek the glory of him who said to me, "I have appointed you to this task

---

18. *Languor*, literally sickness or weariness, also entails "languishing for love."
19. *Dulcor*, a term favored by Richard Rolle.

in order to display my wonders in you—not as in Pharaoh, but as in David and Daniel."[20]

Many people nowadays say, "The Lord has abandoned the earth and does not see us." Some say it in actions, some in words—not literally, but that is their meaning. It is as if they said, "It is neither God's gift nor the spirit of our times to be lovers of God as our fathers were." I answer them, "God is unchanging, and by the nature of his creation, humankind is lovable. So if God gives now just as he did in the past, because he is unchanging and humankind is naturally lovable, I see nothing that could cause the imperfection of those people except their ingratitude. Therefore, to show you that the cause is neither God nor the times, nor anything else but your ingratitude, I will tell you plainly what God has given me to reveal to you."

11. What the purest light of contemplation is like

In the year 1485, the thirty-fourth year of my life and the ninth since I entered the Carthusian Order, while I was in the hermitage of Mount Grace in the province of England, in the diocese of York, the word of the Lord came to me[21] that I might tell you how great is the joy not of the love of the world, but of that health and that sickness that I mentioned before. May our almighty God grant me so to fulfill what he commanded that my word may be a solace to you and a doubled talent to me[22]—not only on my behalf, but also on yours. Let these few words suffice as a prologue; now let the discourse follow.

20. God performed wonders against Pharaoh in the exodus (Exod 6–11, 14–15) not for Pharaoh's benefit, but to manifest his glory. But in the cases of David and Daniel, miracles both glorified God and exalted the Old Testament heroes.

21. A prophetic opening. The biblical prophets commonly name the precise time and place of their calling.

22. Cf. the parable of the talents, Matt 25:14-30.

On the holy day of Easter, which followed the Lord's Annunciation,[23] I was walking outdoors after None in the cloister of my little cell, both asleep and awake as I have explained above. And suddenly the Redeemer's grace was present: a new grace made me rise again, and this is how it happened. Freed somehow from my bodily senses, my mind was raised up to the heights of heaven, and God, to whom nothing is impossible[24] (thanks be to him), ravished me into a marvelous light. Let no one expect me to say what it was like. Yet for his glory's sake, because my purpose requires it, I beg you again and again, readers and hearers: pay attention! I swear before Jesus Christ that I have never related any of these things in a spirit of pride, vainglory, or boastfulness.

That light is the light of health, the light of gladness, the light of a sickness that heals everyone who is ravished into it,[25] yet brings the sufferer close to death through excessive joy, not torment. It was that light that suddenly surrounded me, and I do not know how it came or how it departed.[26] But this I know well: I was within the light, or rather within the source of light.[27] So far as I can understand, the human soul itself is rendered luminous, or rather glorified, to become wholly luminous through absolute righteousness, with nothing left outside it. That light has no end, as I reflected afterward. It is poured out on all sides and at the same time infused into the soul while it is glorified.[28]

---

23. March 25 is the Feast of the Annunciation. Easter in 1485 fell on April 3.

24. Matt 19:26; Luke 1:37.

25. Cf. John 1:9.

26. Cf. John 3:8.

27. *in luce vel pocius in lumine fui.* This subtle distinction recalls Hildegard of Bingen's distinction between the *lux vivens* (living light) and the *umbra viventis lucis* (reflection of the living light), in which she more often saw her visions.

28. *circumfusa est, pariter et infusa.* The concept of infused grace is related to that of infused (as opposed to acquired) virtues, a common distinction in scholastic theology.

12. That the joy of this light is inconceivable

But know this, if you can understand it: the joy of this glorification is not always equal, for the light itself may grow brighter and brighter. Yet no one who has ever truly been caught up in it will believe he could have any greater glory while he remains in the body—until he either reads about or experiences it. To one who has not experienced this, even the least joy is utterly inconceivable. Even one who has experienced it can scarcely conceive of it, not even if he were as mighty as Samson.[29] When the light suddenly comes, it will ravish the chosen one beyond his senses so that later, he can say, "I sleep and my heart is awake." In that moment, he can say nothing at all. But the beloved beloved—that is, the one who is greatly and well beloved—is ravished in this way beyond many others. He may often be ravished, now into the light, now into death itself, in a way, for he sings boldly in spiritual harmony,[30] "I languish for love." Since he is so languid, he is compelled to sit down, or even to lie prostrate on the ground or in bed as he sings without ceasing, "I languish for love." Thanks to the beloved Beloved—the beloved "king of virtues of the beloved Beloved,"[31] as David calls him—I can say this. On Easter day, as I was saying, each time I recovered my strength I was once again brought to the point of death. So I was compelled to sit down and sleep, inebriated by a wondrous sweetness most wondrously mingled with celestial harmony, in a sickness that was delight and not distress.

13. That the man of God should think of sitting down

Such is the way of this luminous celestial joy that, however it may seize the man of God—whatever the time, the place, or the manner

29. Judg 13–16. This hero is not normally linked with mystical experience, but Methley explains his relevance in the last chapter.

30. Divine song or *canor* is a key aspect of Rolle's mysticism as well.

31. Ps 67:13. Methley derives his title from this phrase.

—he should defer to no one, fear no one, and let nothing tear him away, for no one is greater than the man who fears God. It is no wonder if he refuses to forsake that joy for anyone, because God alone can bestow true rapture. At other times, when (unlike other people) he is divinely seized by the languor of distress, or rather delight, he must sit down wherever he may be, provided that the place would not be dangerous or scandalous. But in fact, he always has the special help of God, so whether he is inside or out, it will be an occasion not of scandal, but of virtue. As I said before, his neighbor is helped by God. That is why I am not compelled to rest during Mass, but rather in the peace of my cell, on the ground, or in my prayer stall, or even on the grass in the garden, as I sing and languish. Would that I could languish no longer, but die of mourning in a moment or, better, pass from the death of this present life to the glory that shall be!

The man of God does not care about time, for just when he expects to be chanting psalms, strolling in the open air at midday, he may be subjected for a long while to this death, rather than the pleasure of the garden. That is what happened to me the day before yesterday. Yet I am compelled to use this time not for pleasure, but to preserve my health. Indeed, when I go to bed at midnight or in the evening, still dressed in my daytime habit or almost naked in my woolen underwear,[32] if the beloved Beloved inflicts a single blow of that most languishing delight, I am compelled to languish and sing even more than before. But why should I ramble on with many words? Let no one think I can by any means explain how great is the joy of that health—or that sickness. It is enough to believe that this experience is more than human.

---

32. *vestitus diurnalibus seu stamineis fere nudus.* Methley's intimacy with the reader is striking.

14. That nothing is safer than to have no fear, even when one is afraid

One who desires to sleep continually can find nothing safer than to have no fear. I dare say that if nothing stands in the way, someone whose heart is drawn by heaven to entrust himself wholly to God cannot perish. But he must trust God even in doubtful or dangerous matters, when the outcome remains unclear in spite of counsel and scriptural aid. For nothing is safer than to have no fear, even when one is afraid. One who dares not fear cannot be troubled.[33] "As for me, I am poor and needy," I say, "but the Lord cares for me. You are my helper and my protector, O my God, do not delay."[34] What does that mean? Because I languish for love, it is fitting and right for you to call me with your holy call from this world to yourself, through yourself, and for yourself, in your altogether surpassing love, by every good way that is possible, inasmuch as all creation is united with you in its degree. According to my small measure, how can I think to set an example of holiness for the whole world, to convert the world to your perpetual praise and satisfy the desire of my heart in your love and good zeal? For I sleep and my heart is awake, and I languish greatly for love.

15. Why the heart is said to be awake

Why is it said "I sleep and my heart is awake," rather than "I sleep and I am awake"? Let no one doubt that there is a reason. Within my heart, the violence of love is so great that even though my body and soul are filled through and through with celestial delight, yet because of this surpassing violence in my heart, I am forced

---

33. *Qui non audet timere, turbari non potest.* A memorable aphorism.
34. Ps 39:18.

to melt like wax before the fire.[35] My physical heart seems to be dancing in my breast, moving as if it could lift my body by that means and present itself intimately to heaven, heart and body together. Failing that, it longs to leave the body behind and appear weightless before God, all by itself. For I feel in my breast that when my heart cannot carry my whole body with itself through the airy spaces, it strives to break free and leap out with great violence, in a rush of sweetness, with immense jubilation. And so I rightly say as I cry out and sing, "I sleep and my heart is awake."

16. What it meant when Saint John the Evangelist played with the bird[36]

Why is it better to feel divine love constantly, every day, than to overflow with a few little tears in rare moments, when the heart may be contrite yet tears of love are lacking? What theologian, no matter how right he is in other respects, dares deny that such a state can be achieved? The theologian cites Saint John the Evangelist as an example, yet he does not understand his case. Scripture says of the contemplative life with eternal Wisdom that "her companionship has no bitterness, nor her company tedium, but joy and gladness."[37]

John's words are lofty, but certainly not false. Lest he become a scandal or a bad example for such people, I will explain briefly who can be touched by divine Wisdom. It is the person who is not full of carnal desires like a lecher, but is often enveloped by light.

---

35. Ps 21:15.

36. In John Cassian's *Conferences* 24.21, Saint John the Evangelist strokes a partridge for recreation, noting that even the most contemplative mind must sometimes relax its rigor to avoid self-destruction. This text was deeply familiar to monks because it is recommended in the Benedictine Rule, chap. 73.

37. Wis 8:16. Cf. Henry Suso, *Horologium Sapientiae* 1.1, which underlies much of this chapter. Suso argues with an unnamed scholastic theologian. An English adaptation, *The Treatise of the Seven Points of True Love and Everlasting Wisdom*, was probably composed at Mount Grace.

Praise to the Creator! There are some who often study the creation, such as natural philosophers, physicians, and scientists,[38] yet they are far from devotion. Let them look to the present case; I am not speaking to them. Others stir up devotion by contemplating the creation, like the new monastic disciples of Christ and those who dwell in the desert. Yet sometimes they can find no devotion by that means, so they lament that they are touched (or rather overcome) by ennui. John is not one of those! Still others, like the heavenly men who are illumined by the whole of Scripture as well as the creation, often rise in the way I have described to a love so great that they are ravished beyond themselves. Sometimes they almost die from an excess of languishing love, while at other times they are more sober; yet they always abound in celestial light. Among these is John, together with those who daily and continually feel some kind of perceptible, affective love—though not always to the same degree.

17. On the perceptible qualities of love,[39] and that no one is excluded from the love of God

Those who wish to enjoy continual devotion should never entrust themselves to the consolation of a creature, if they can by any other means escape a mortal temptation. Some say that to feel a perceptible devotion is a special gift of God, and I agree: nothing is truer. But you in turn, hear what I say—or rather, this is what Scripture says, so I say it too. "This only have I found," Ecclesiastes says. "God made humanity righteous; but people have meddled in infinite questions."[40] If man in general is righteous, then he is by nature lovable, both actively and passively—that is, able

---

38. *phisici medicive seu studentes vniuersitate nature.*

39. *De sensibilitatibus amoris. Sentio, sensibilis,* and *sensibiliter* are keywords for Methley, denoting a combination of warm feeling and palpable sense perception. No English term is a precise equivalent.

40. Eccl 7:30.

to love and be loved. Consider an analogy. What man or woman does not love someone, male or female, with more affection than others? So if you feel such perceptible affection for a creature, you can transfer it to God in a suitable way. I promise you on his behalf that you will have a special gift—a perceptible, indeed tangible, love.

Listen, you lovers of the world, listen to me! Taking God and my conscience to witness, I swear that the fire of love, like a perfume, can be perceived by the senses in its surpassing sweetness. It can be recognized as easily as we distinguish between cold in winter and heat in summer. As for angelic song,[41] it is just as real in true lovers as a secular tune sung by teenagers in the flower of their youth. Just as one can be known, so can the other. Who has ever heard or read of anyone who truly, totally entrusted himself to divine love without possessing this special gift? So it is clear beyond doubt: no one who gives himself wholly to the grace of God is excluded.

18. On venial sins and the cause of ennui

We read that there were gnats in the land of Egypt.[42] Gnats are tiny flies, and what do they signify but the horde of venial sins—the tiniest offenses? Even if you cannot avoid all sins, you will gradually attain such purity of mind that you would not knowingly commit even the smallest sin, because even if it were permitted, you would not want to commit it. These flies are not mortal sins, but they are doubtless the reason we do not feel perceptible, continual devotion all day long.

Some might say that sin is not always the cause of intolerable ennui. Yet we must explain this so that ennui does not again become a cause of sin. Consider two people. One is tested to see if he would want to attain the love of the world if it were permitted.

41. *Canor angelicus*, again reminiscent of Rolle.
42. Exod 8:16-19.

Such a person feels no inner ennui because he has no desire for that love; he is truly dead to it. The second is taught to bear it patiently when ennui afflicts him from time to time. The first person endures this trial for no reason except original sin and wins a crown of greater glory in heaven, both on his own behalf and on God's. Doubtless the second has not yet done full penance for his sins to purify his affections, even if he has obeyed all the injunctions of his confessor. Though he committed no actual sin at that time, his previous sin is incompletely purged, as I have said.[43] But if he has labored perfectly, he will be liberated promptly. Afterward he will enjoy glory in God so great that he could not continue to live in the flesh, unless God's protection preserved the one he created in the first place. Thanks be to him forever—for in this way I sleep and my heart is awake.

19. On the song and canticle at dawn

O Jesu Jesu Jesu![44] Jesu Jesu Jesu! Jesu Jesu Jesu! I languish for love and rejoice at heart, or rather I dance for surpassing joy. Jesu Jesu Jesu! By your precious blood, by your glorious passion, by your bitter, bitter, bitter death, by the glorious assumption of your mother and mine, I beg you to receive my spirit, for I languish for love.[45] Such are the lyrics of the canticle I sing, but I can scarcely conceive of its music except by inserting a bit in my prose. Since you have given me a special gift—Jesu Jesu Jesu!—I ask in union with you, invoking all that can possibly please you: Receive my spirit, for I languish for love.

43. Methley's explanation of why even a monk in a state of grace sometimes suffers from *acedia*, boredom or dryness in prayer.

44. Like Rolle, Methley frequently uses the prayer of the Holy Name. Meant for contemplative oral recitation, this prayer works best with open vowels, so I have used the archaic English vocative *Jesu*, which is close to the Latin *Iesu*. The ninefold repetition suggests the Trinity and the nine angelic orders.

45. Acts 7:58, Song 2:5. For the next several chapters, Methley expresses his frustration that he cannot die at once and be united with God forever.

In this way, rising suddenly at dawn, I offer heaven the first fruits of my thoughts and words. The devil does not hold me captive to ennui or slumber, but the minute I wake, I intone this song and canticle, which I sing with honey-sweet languor, not grieving pain. But what shall I say about the words I set down, namely *precious, glorious, bitter*? I sing these three words especially because I can neither explain nor understand how deeply I taste them in my heart. When I say "by your bitter death," I am forced by the excess of languishing love to repeat the word *bitter*, saying, "by your bitter, bitter, O bitter, O bitter, bitter death,[46] I beg to be dissolved and be with Christ."[47] And it is the same when I say "by your precious blood" and "by your glorious passion." In this way my heart is awake, and I sleep.

20. A debate between two sleepers in one bed

I know that you have come to dispute or even debate with me. But a slave never disputes or debates with his master and departs without guilt. You well know, Lord, that you are asking for a debate, so I will answer you, since you promise or rather inspire me to do this.

I know very well that you are speaking to me about yourself when you say, "I sleep and my heart wakes for you." Because you are asleep, I cry, "Why you do not listen to me?"

"I hear your cry! It is impossible for me not to grant what you ask. But I want you to desire it still more ardently."

"More ardently, Lord, more ardently! If any should think me to blame and judge me for it, let them hear how I cry and judge between me and you."

"I am never unaware of what or how you cry."

---

46. *Per amaram, amaram, O amaram, O amaram, amaram mortem tuam.* The phrase is chantlike—an alliterative mantra.
47. Phil 1:23.

"It would be very strange, Lord, if you were unaware, since we both sleep in one bed. But I ask you, let me debate with you so that those who do not know which side to take can judge. This is how I cry: 'O Lord, hear my prayer, and let my cry come unto you.'[48] When I say 'my cry,' I feel more perceptible desire in my heart than I can express or even imagine. O let my cry, Lord, let my cry come unto you!"

"What have you to do with me,[49] that you should cry to me?"

"It is because you are my joy, Lord, and I can have nothing else. For love compels me to feel so much desire for you that I want to love nothing else, even if it were allowed—which it is not. Even if what I feel for you is not much, listen to me anyhow, for by an act of will I think I can miraculously compel you. So I ask by the depths of your sweet heart; by your heart's sweet blood I beg you! I knock, I ask, I seek[50]—and indeed, in measureless love I often command you and adjure you:[51] Receive me, for I languish for love."

And the Lord replies, "What are you saying?" The Lord replies: "I answer you and say, I sleep and my heart wakes for you." Thus says the Lord.

21. A second debate, and on the secret judgment

I sleep, Lord, for your left hand is under my head and your right hand will embrace me.[52] In a way, it embraces me even now. But to awaken you, I will knock on your side and say to you, my beloved Beloved, "Jesu Jesu Jesu! Jesu Jesu Jesu! Jesu Jesu Jesu, hear my cry! Jesu Jesu Jesu! Jesu Jesu Jesu! Jesu Jesu Jesu, wake up and receive my spirit. Jesu Jesu Jesu! Jesu Jesu Jesu! Jesu Jesu

---

48. Ps 101:2, a prayer used frequently in the Divine Office.
49. John 2:4, Jesus' words to Mary at the wedding in Cana.
50. Cf. Matt 7:7.
51. Song 1:7.
52. Song 2:6.

Jesu! My heart's cry seems to fill heaven and earth because of my surpassing desire to be dissolved and be with you.[53] Yet still you sleep and do not listen."

"Can it ever happen," the Lord asks, "that I, who gave you this desire, will not listen to a cry that surely pleased me even before it came out of your mouth?"

"Jesu Jesu Jesu! Jesu Jesu Jesu! Jesu Jesu Jesu, it comes out of my heart!"

"And it enters my heart."

"Lord, why do you make me wait? Look, I beg you by the glorious assumption of your mother and mine, for it pleases her as well as you that you should listen to me."

"And should I, who granted you this prayer, not listen to her as well as you?"

"But why do you delay, Lord?"

"Because I sent you into the field to reap, or rather to bring in the harvest and the sheaves,[54] and now you want to come and leave some of those sheaves in the field. This cannot be! First gather all your works, your virtues, and your desires—and then you will come to me."

"Jesu Jesu Jesu! Jesu Jesu Jesu! Jesu Jesu Jesu, do not force me to linger in the world. I seek not honor but love."

"And why should I obey you, when for the same reason I made even my mother wait after my ascension?"

"Still, I will continue to dispute and debate with you. Who would dare say that the doctors of the Church, such as Augustine, Jerome, and Ambrose, would not have done even more good works in body and spirit if they had lived longer? Yet you called them from the world to yourself. True, I know that the reasoning you have laid down is just, not wicked. At least in your secret judg-

---

53. Phil 1:23.
54. Cf. Matt 9:37-38.

ment, which you alone know, it doubtless redounds to your honor and my reward."

22. *How by turns they sleep and wake for one another*

"But again, hear how I contend with you. I know you listen to your mother, who is my adoptive mother, and you honor her in all things. Last night I saw her in a spiritual illumination, and I specially urged her above all creatures, by virtue of loving obedience, to promote my cause with you as far as it was permitted and possible. I am sure she heard my prayer, and therefore she has prayed to you on my behalf. If you want to settle the question this way, you will say, 'I have not listened to her. Be quiet, then, and say no more about this'—until you will."

Say, "Lord, until you will."[55]

"I also know, Richard, my beloved beloved, that you want what I want. And now I tell you that I did heed your prayer—and that of your mother and mine. But when it will be granted, you cannot hear, because you cannot bear delay."

"Jesu Jesu Jesu! Jesu Jesu Jesu, for your own sake! O my God! O O O Jesu Jesu Jesu! For your own sake, my God, attend and do not delay, for I sleep and my heart wakes for you. And surely, even though you may be asleep because you keep me waiting, your heart wakes for me."

23. *How love has no limit, and about a rapture*

I will sing no mournful song, no lamentations and woes. No, I will sing Alleluia, for I have found what I sought in the desert—not in the same way I did at first, but newly restored by the Beloved. Jesu Jesu Jesu! I sleep and my heart wakes for you. If only you would complete what you began last night!

55. Or "Lord, say 'until you will.'" The MS reflects some confusion about who is speaking at this point.

What might that be? Thanks to you, I can say that I am like a spring of living water whose streams pour forth limpid waters,[56] so long as they are not blocked or obstructed. When the waters begin to dry up, they seem to have reached their limit. But later, someone returns for a drink and finds that the channel he had left empty is full again. So it is in me. Your love can never be exhausted as long as you continue to bestow grace, as you have done until this hour. Thanks to you, I have never yet obstructed the streams.

Jesu Jesu Jesu! Jesu Jesu Jesu! Jesu Jesu Jesu! As you revealed to me last night, you keep ingratitude from blocking the waters and overcoming me. I have learned from experience that I can die, and I think my death will be without distress, though not without delight. For I experienced death almost to the point of breathing my last, or so it seemed to me—yet I did not actually die.[57] Suddenly you ravished me above myself in the spirit. This happened three or four times in an hour, as I returned to myself again and again. Because I so often felt such a great and unexpected joy, yet you kept me from actual death, I thought of the Scripture verse, "the Son of Man will come at an hour you do not expect."[58] But if I am to leave this world and go to you at an hour I do not expect—and you also are coming to me, you whom I await with such strong desire, as you know—there is nothing better than to live well at all times, never ceasing to await you and desire you.

24. *On the condition of those who die of excessive love*

If anyone wonders what it is like for a lover to feel drawn upward by the greatness of love or its extreme violence, I say he must learn from experience, if he wants to know fully. Yet I can say that anyone who is like me (though in my own judgment, I am but a

---

56. Cf. Jer 2:13; 17:13.

57. *sed non contigit totaliter spiritum emittere*; cf. Matt 27:50. Julian of Norwich reports a similar near-death experience in *A Revelation of Love*, chap. 3.

58. Luke 12:40.

worm compared to the saints of old)—such a person will feel, in spirit and body, like a beggar at a rich man's door.[59] The beggar expects or rather hopes to receive alms at any moment, because he has heard that the lord will soon be going out. Yet he sometimes happens to be intent on something else, such as prayer or meditation. While he is so occupied, not thinking at that moment that the lord may emerge from his house or castle, yet having a habitual desire—the lord may indeed go out and give him alms.

Some might prefer a different analogy. If a prisoner knows that the king is coming to set him free, who can describe his desire as he waits for him? When the king arrives, who can imagine the prisoner's joy as he walks free? Yet all such analogies fall short in one respect. I do not wait for God for any reason but himself, even though I may abound with him in all the goods of creation. The beggar and the prisoner, on the other hand, rejoice in his coming out of love for their own welfare.

Even before I was ravished into the light at the time I mentioned, I was already overflowing with the greatest joy. Having in a way become angelic, I enjoyed jubilant song and the most languishing love, with a vision of God even clearer than the frequent visitations of the rapture I described.

25. On compassion and perceptible affection

Last night, on the day after the feast of Saints Tiburtius, Valerian, and Maximus,[60] I received a celestial illumination in the spirit. You told me, Lord God, that I should lovingly ask which of us feels greater compassion for the other, and which of us is affected more perceptibly by the other's love. You said this because I had asked, "Where is your compassion for me, my God, since I am kept for your sake in such torments of languishing love?" This is surely a pleasant topic, but exploring it requires great intelligence

---

59. Cf. the parable of Dives and Lazarus: Luke 16:19-31.
60. The feast falls on April 14.

or celestial illumination. Since you were the first to raise the question, grant me grace not to fall beneath the burden.

To put it briefly, it accords with our faith that you undoubtedly feel greater compassion and affection for me. But you want me to explain this more clearly with your help. So I will begin my argument this way: You love me and I love you. When two companions share a bed, it is their habit that when one of them wants anything, they both want it. But my wish is to come to you, see you, hold you, and never let you go in heaven.[61] I cannot separate my own body from my soul to come to you, for it was not I who joined them or created them. But you can, beyond a doubt, for you did create them. Again, no one else can release me without your help. Who then is to blame, I ask? Tell me!

Yes, I know what you are saying: it is sin [that keeps me from you]. But you did not specify if it is original or actual sin. You did not resolve the difficulty of the question. But I trust you will resolve it later and clarify what I have not yet explained about perceptible affection and delightful compassion.

26. That Christ's compassion and desire are greater than ours

"I can and will release you, O man, have no doubt. But you do not know when."

"I do know, Lord, because you told me for certain that I will soon come to you."

"I did not set any hour or moment. But since it is sure to happen, let us talk about the compassion of love (for you suffer pain that I might have glory), and your own compassion and suffering. I, the Lord, can no longer suffer pain in my own body, which is glorified. But you cannot imagine how great is my desire for you. Because of that desire, I feel for you a compassion that is almost sensual.[62] Your salvation is not impeded because I can no longer

---

61. Cf. Song 3:4.

62. *compassionem quasi sensibilem.*

suffer pain. You see then that I have a perceptible feeling or affection for you, as well as a compassion free from pain—which is fitting, since I am immortal."

"Lord, let us see if I can understand this. Although you love me more than I love you, why do you not want to release me yet so that I can come to you, see you, hold you, and never let you go?"

"Listen, my beloved beloved! 'I have set my eyes on you in the road you are walking, and my ears hearken to your prayers,' as the prophet says.[63] If you are righteous, you be the judge, with your conscience as witness. Is your own righteousness the cause of this?"

"What mortal, Lord, is righteous by his own effort without your grace? I know I am a sinner. Your grace to me is immense, for you deign to set your eyes on me in goodness for love's sake, according to the prophetic verse you cited. But since you said that your ears hearken to my prayers, I ask, or rather I beg you, beloved Beloved: reveal how this can be."

27. What is needed to maintain perfection

"I revealed that to you through the psalmist, beloved beloved, when he told you how to attend to me: 'My eyes are always on the Lord, for he will release my feet from the snare.' "[64]

"Lord God, what mortal always has his eyes on you or open to you? Yet I suppose the psalmist offered counsel as well as a remedy, so I could know what is needed to maintain perfection."

"I want your eyes to be on me at all times as far as possible, O man, just as mine are on you—until I say, 'Turn your eyes from me, for they have made me fly away.'[65] Turn the eyes of your body and soul toward me until your contemplation is perfect—but then turn them away from me. Yet you will still see me with one

63. Ps 31:8; 33:16.
64. Ps 24:15.
65. Song 6:4.

eye—the eye of unknown affection, which surpasses all others. Thus, as far as possible, we will have equal compassion and perceptible affection. But there will never be complete equality in our single bed."

"That is because of my smallness, Lord, for I cannot match you in desire. Clearly, you have greater compassion in your way, as well as greater affection for me, than I have for you."

28. How the eyes will always be on the Lord

"But what shall I say? Listen carefully. You said, 'let your eyes be on me at all times—yet turn them away from me in contemplation, for you will be wounded by one of my eyes because we love one another.'[66] I have learned from experience (if I have fully understood) that if I were constantly intent on the purest contemplation, never ceasing, neglecting all else except what is due to my vows, I would soon die of excessive fervor, for my heart would totally melt within me.[67] So I sometimes devote myself to meditation, vocal prayer, and other things so I will not be dissolved by my own hand or effort, but rather by yours.

"But I also say this. If I constantly *desired* to die in this manner, as indeed I do almost without ceasing, once again I would soon die of excessive desire. For I languish violently for surpassing love! With inconceivable desire I call upon your name, Jesus, more times than I have hairs on my head.[68] Now I will pose a question. If I am lifted up to you with so great an affection by such means, why then should I turn my eyes (or at least one of them) away from you? For you never turn yours away from me, having set them on me with so great a love. Now speak, Lord, for it was you who first posed this question."

---

66. Cf. Song 4:9.
67. Cf. Ps 21:15.
68. Cf. Ps 39:13.

The Lord says, "A human mind, free from such toil, cannot be wearied by thinking about me. So think about me with reverence and devotion at every moment, and you will not harm your body or soul in any way. And thus your eyes, that is, your spiritual gaze, will be on me just as mine is on you."

29. The response and conclusion of the debate between God and man

"Now, Lord, I clearly see the answer to my previous question. You said it was because of sin that you do not dissolve me and let me come to you, for you surely seek to find righteousness in me. But still I dispute with you, for man never remains in the same state,[69] yet you seek to find me totally pure of sin. Forgive me freely, then, because you are good—and receive my spirit, for it was you who gave it. What shall I say? At least hear me now: by no means am I seeking honor, but love. Surely you too seek love, I dare say! But what about honor? Surely you have shown me what to say. 'I will deliver you and you will honor me,' says the prophet.[70] And again, 'A sacrifice of praise will honor me.'[71] I dare say you want to be honored not because of wicked pride, but for your divine creative nature, if I can understand this by analogy.

"But that is not the question I asked. My question is this: Because you are able to set me free; because you love me; because you are not unaware of sin, knowing that it stands in the way; and because no one in the world lives without sin[72]—why then do you wait for me to be free of sin, even though you and I both desire nothing from one another but love? True, you also desire honor, but that is because of your divine nature. I know how you speak, and you are speaking to me even now in the spirit. But please do

69. Job 14:2.
70. Ps 49:15.
71. Ps 49:23.
72. Cf. 1 John 1:8.

not be angry if I still debate with you, for I languish for love! Surely it is not for accidental reasons that you love me and I love you. Rather, your own love is the reason. So because accidental qualities cannot perfect me, nor can I ever be free of them, I simply cannot understand why, on their account, you want to delay my coming to you.[73] For I am sure that anyone who languishes for pure love, seeking no other reward, denies nothing to the beloved."

"O beloved beloved, how long will you argue and debate with me? Again and again I have told you in the spirit that you cannot penetrate this mystery. But hold firmly to this truth: you are a sinner, and you are not yet ready—partly because of original sin, partly because of actual sin—even though the sacraments are real and you have received them. Further, I have foreknown and fore-ordained the precise moment when you will put off your body, and it cannot be passed over. You will undoubtedly leave this world and come to me at the very best time, all things considered. So be patient, vanquish your vices, and I will give you grace. Love fervently and I will crown you. Persist in your chaste desire and you will be victorious, never vanquished by the devil. Finally, bear in mind that there is nothing in you, however small—whether good or evil—that will not receive its reward."

30. A consolation for God's delay

"I thought I had found a companion on a bed of flowers.[74] Yet now you want to leave me, abandoning me to danger and deferring the petition you inspired. 'I will not leave you nor abandon you,'[75] for I languish for love!"

---

73. Drawing on Thomist metaphysics, Methley argues (speciously) that sin does not belong to the substance of the soul, but is merely an accident, contingent and changeable. God should therefore not postpone his death—and anticipated beatitude—because of it.

74. Song 1:15.

75. Josh 1:5.

"I in turn say the same to you, mortal."[76]

"Lord, if only you had taken me from this world without delay, before you resolved the question and thrust me away like this!"

"Mortal, nothing I have said can hinder you. I told you in fact that you cannot resolve this question. Yet I did not deny what I promised you last year, namely that after you finish the book called *The Cellar* you will come to me, and I will console you."[77]

"Lord, there is absolutely no way (saving your will) except by the death I am awaiting."

"Mortal, when you are at the summit of your mind,[78] I can still ravish you whenever I want. And at that moment you are without sin, as Scripture says, because 'nothing defiled enters into' contemplation.[79] Therefore sin will not hinder you."

"O beloved Beloved! If my foreordained time will not hinder me either, it seems that what you said above will not be able to delay me. For once, at least, give me a good and auspicious answer now!"

"O mortal! I showed you in the spirit that I can accomplish what I will in due time. As for my promise, there is nothing false about it, whether your days turn out to be few or many, for I can fulfill my promise however and whenever I wish—and the same holds true for everyone."

"Because your wisdom has no limit,[80] Lord, it is no wonder that you have prolonged the lives of some people and shortened those of others. Who can blame you? Indeed, the book of Daniel

---

76. *O homo*, used throughout this dialogue. The term is singular, personal, and gender-neutral.

77. A lost work written in 1484. Methley seems to have written a book inspired by each space in the monastery: the school, the cellar, the refectory, and the dormitory. But Carthusians do not have all these spaces.

78. *in supremo mentis apice*, a technical term for the part of the soul engaged in pure contemplation. Methley's "consolation" is that, even if he cannot yet be fully united with God in death, he can enjoy the temporary union of rapture.

79. Wis 7:25.

80. Ps 146:5.

says that 'seventy weeks have been shortened upon your people.'[81]
So this is how you have consoled me: my sin can be erased by
contemplation and the time can be shortened by your providence,
for 'a thousand years in your sight are like yesterday when it has
passed.'[82] As I well see, nothing can resist you, for you can both
preserve your truth and shorten the time.[83] You can surely call
me at this moment, as well as at any time this year or in the future.
So your consolation is a good one—and moreover, it is true. But
if only you would fulfill your promise without delay!"

"Mortal, I will tell you how to be consoled. Apart from my
hidden judgment, it is up to you whether you are kept away from
me for a short time or a long one. Labor fervently and never
withdraw your mind from me while you are awake—and very
soon you will be presented to me to rejoice without end."

31. What should be done about constant troubles

"I am never free from some kind of trouble, so how can I be awake
for you and asleep to the world? It is a great feat, a very great one,
to have constant troubles (and I mean constant!), yet never withdraw one's mind from God in waking life."

"O man, I bid you answer your God. What do you do against
this constant trouble?"

"Your will be done.[84] Above all, I love you and give you thanks,
simply for your own sake and, if possible, without accidental
reasons. See, I have spoken briefly."

"Explain at greater length."

81. Dan 9:24.

82. Ps 89:4.

83. This resolution recalls a similar paradox in Julian of Norwich: God can both
preserve the truth of Scripture, or "save [his] word in all things" (i.e., that some will
be damned), and fulfill his promise to her (that "all manner of thing shall be well").
A Revelation of Love, chap. 32.

84. Matt 6:10, the Lord's Prayer.

"O Lord, my beloved Beloved, I will speak. I know that all things work together for good for those who are called to be saints according to your purpose.[85] So I do not care about the fate of the world or any accidental thing, so long as I am not the cause of any evil. But in general, I always do what is best (not merely what is good) according to my own judgment, after fully considering all the circumstances as one should. I am certain, because I have learned from experience, that no sooner is one trouble removed than another arises, worse than the first. By such means it pleases you to test a person you love (who also loves you) until he is mortified in every way. That is why it is a waste of time to say, 'When this or that trouble is over, I will be at peace.'"

"O man, why do you consent to the devil? Sow your seed in the morning and do not cease in the evening, for you do not know which will spring up sooner.[86] Do you want to know something more important? Without action, the monastic habit is damnable. If you do not double the talent entrusted to you, what account will you render to the just judge?[87] So, whatever good you have received in your words and your habit, you must perfect in action and in love."

You contemplatives, all you who wear a clerical or monastic habit, but put on an altogether worldly crown in your actions [. . .].[88] Along with the tonsure, these things are symbols of contemplation. So if you want to have continual peace, remain calm in all situations. Do nothing at all with your body or mind except what can help you acquire or preserve peace of mind, according to God and your order. Thanks to God, I have such peace not just for a moment, as scoffers say, but constantly.[89] There is

---

85. Rom 8:28.
86. Eccl 11:6.
87. Matt 25:22-23; Luke 16:2.
88. Some words appear to be missing at this point.
89. A persistent debate revolves around whether exalted states of union or contemplative peace can be attained permanently or only in passing. Methley, like Marguerite Porete, takes the first view.

never a moment when I do not rejoice in the Beloved. Undoubt-edly, though, a person who knowingly or willingly takes any de-light in the world, rightly or wrongly, hopes in vain to be filled with heavenly delights to his heart's content. But I must explain why I said "rightly or wrongly." Such pleasure can be right insofar as it is sometimes promised to people as a way to avoid a greater evil. I said "wrongly" because sin must be avoided.

32. On the compositions of holy men through the Holy Spirit

But why, my Beloved, do we dwell on these things? They are as far from the solitary man as the east is from the west.[90] Let our talk be about love, which dwells freely in lovers and always gives a writer new material. Just as God has no measure, his love cannot be measured or limited in anyone who is ruled by the Spirit of God,[91] so long as grace is present. That is why those who discuss perceptible love rarely scrutinize the words of others or cite stan-dard authorities. Nor do they organize their writings in the usual way, setting up divisions and subdivisions, for the Holy Spirit knows what a reader may unexpectedly need.[92] So the Spirit ar-ranges a book more as a doctor treats a patient, not as a court chef cooks for a hungry diner. At court people usually share the same taste. But when it suits the Holy Spirit to make distinctions within his exhortations, the man of God acquiesces and serves the Spirit's plan, rather than catering to curious tastes. For this reason the holy fathers, who are now in heaven praising God, wrote their sermons differently than preachers today, although both methods are good.[93]

---

90. Ps 102:12.

91. Cf. Bernard of Clairvaux, *De diligendo Deo* 1.1: "God himself is the reason why he is to be loved. As for how he is to be loved, there is to be no limit to that love."

92. *sciens quid inopinate occurrat necessitatem paciendi presencia quondam lectura*. The text is garbled.

93. Methley's apologia for his unorthodox method of composition. The point of this analogy is that a doctor tailors his prescriptions to each patient's individual need,

This is the way I also write, for (thanks be to God!) I continually sleep and my heart wakes for you. O Jesu Jesu, beloved Beloved! The book or sermon I am writing for you is not my own, but yours. In the next chapter there is a dish to be set before everyone, a course of heavenly sweetness. But I want you, my students, to know that these words are not mine. They are the words of Eternal Wisdom, who is Christ—for the Lord has revealed to me in the spirit what I shall tell you.[94]

I wrote this passage on Saturday before the Sunday when we sing the Office, "The earth is full of the Lord's mercy."[95] On Monday, I resumed writing in the same chapter where I had left off with the words "For the Lord has revealed to me." Because the Holy Spirit dictated what I wrote on Saturday, I promised something without knowing what it would be. Yet it was God who directed my pen, not I myself, so he who promised this heavenly dish through my writing fulfilled his promise afterward in this way.

33. A spiritual vision of the heavenly dish

On Monday I was mindful of that dish of heavenly sweetness that God had promised me as I said Sext for the day and Nones of our Lady. Afterward I sat alone for a while, wondering if I had done everything well. Suddenly I looked up at the crucifix, and at once I entered a state of spiritual illumination. And lo! I saw the Lord Jesus Christ standing on top of a very high mountain, so high that I marveled. As I gazed into the face of my Christ because I especially love him (but without despising others), I saw what he

---

while a court chef prepares the same deluxe meal for everyone. Patristic preaching, inspired by the Holy Spirit, lacks the precise, rigid organization of scholastic sermons in Methley's day.

94. A reminiscence of Henry Suso's *Horologium Sapientiae*, which presents Christ under the feminine figure of Eternal Wisdom (Prov 8; Sir 24).

95. Ps 32:5. The opening words of the Divine Office for the second Sunday after Easter.

wanted. He was standing on the mountaintop so he could see a long way, and he longed to receive a gift that I will explain below. I knew this without a word because, as I said, I saw what he desired. So I asked him in spirit, "Lord, what do you want to have? Is it my heart?"

"Yes," he said, "I want your heart." This voice sounded not in words but in my understanding, which was illumined. At once I grasped my chest on both sides with both hands and offered him what he most desired—my heart. In fact, he already had it, but he wants to have it more and more fully as long as I live, because no one is so perfect that he cannot be perfected still more. His desire did not spring from any need, but from a true and altogether gracious will down to the last degree. Moreover, his desire had no measure; it was above all measure. He was so lovely to look at, though he was crucified and bloody, that the sight of him feeds a lover with inconceivable delights. When I offered him my heart, he received it most graciously, as if it were a heavenly dish or an angelic service.[96] At once I fully returned to myself—and languished for love.

This was my vision, and here is my exhortation to you who love God, not the world. If you want to have this heavenly dish, let your heart be truly (which means totally) offered to God. Believe me, for both you and God it will have more savor than all spices. Then he will surely forgive your sin by his grace and pour his love into you, so that every one of you may say, "I languish for love," and "I sleep and my heart is awake."

---

96. This vision recalls Mechthild of Hackeborn, *Liber specialis gratiae* 7.11; see also 1.23 and 2.23. The *Speculum devotorum*, an English Carthusian text (ca. 1420–1440), recommends Mechthild as one of three "approved women," along with Birgitta of Sweden and Catherine of Siena. English Carthusians also diffused a Middle English translation, *The Booke of Gostlye Grace*.

34. How lovers share everything in common

Listen to still more about this dish of happiness, for the one who brings it to you is not lessened by laying a table, nor wearied by serving, nor exhausted by writing. He can never be poor and his beloved Beloved can never be a beggar, so long as grace endures in them both. To be sure, everyone is a beggar before God. But lovers share everything in common, so a true lover is endowed with whatever he needs. God will provide for him just as surely as he has no lack, but abounds in all things. These goods are kept all the more securely because they are under God's control, not man's, and God can lose nothing. Moreover, lover and beloved exchange gifts so frequently that if one of them has anything, the other will soon have it as well.[97] As for this dish of heavenly sweetness that I have described: God himself is what he has,[98] and he has what he is in himself, without regard for creatures. When he gives the contemplative a perfect gift, therefore, he gives himself and so justifies himself. In addition he gives virtues, forgiving guilt but fully justifying himself, according to a person's way of life.[99] That is why I say: I sleep with him in bed and my heart is awake, for I languish for love.

Clearly, then, lovers share everything. I say "lovers" and not the world because in the world, where envy reigns supreme, almost nothing is shared. Even when it is, it is shared under false colors so that people can cheat each other. So if anyone is already rich in virtues and wants to be sated with this dish of heavenly sweetness, let him be content with nothing but God—no angel,

---

97. The free exchange of gifts between lover and beloved is an important theme in Marguerite Porete's *Mirror of Simple Souls*; see for instance chaps. 30, 43, and 118 (the third state). Methley translated the *Mirror* into Latin from a Middle English version, itself a translation from the original French.

98. Cf. Augustine, *De civitate Dei* 11.10.3: *quae habet, haec et est* (PL 41:327).

99. *secundum vie modum*; reading *vite* for MS *vie*. For God's self-justification, see Ps 50:6 and Rom 3:4.

no mortal, no saint, no creature at all. Let the person who is always discreet go quite mad in contemplation! Let him dream while he is wide awake, until nothing but God can ever give him delight.

35. *What the food of the heavenly country is like*

That is why I want to refresh you with the food of charity, if you desire to sleep in this sweet slumber. After you have been refreshed as fully as the present life allows,[100] you will yearn for sleep. So then you will not lie awake in bed for very long, but swiftly and without delay, the bed of flowers will embrace you and sleep will seize your eyes. Understand, if you can, that these things should be understood spiritually. If you have not yet tasted them, listen to a few hints so you may know what the food of the heavenly country tastes like. This is that food of which David the psalmist sings: "in a voice of exultation and praise, the sound of feasting."[101]

Last night I promised to explain what the food of the heavenly country is like, but the bell for Vespers of the blessed Virgin Mother of God kept me from going beyond the passage that begins "in a voice."[102] When I made that promise, I did not yet know what I was promising. But I did know that God wanted me to write as I did, so he himself has fulfilled what I promised. After I had said Vespers, as I recall, I was genuflecting at the antiphon *Salve Regina* when suddenly, in an instant, that heavenly food snatched me out of my bodily senses. Insofar as I can now grasp that illumination, I enjoyed the same state (despite my smallness) that we will have in glory, in the glorified body. Let no one think I can explain how utterly removed I was from all things that pass away.

---

100. *provt via presens patitur*; again reading *vita* for MS *via*.
101. Ps 41:5.
102. Methley was writing, not preaching, but he follows Saint Bernard's custom (in his *Sermons on the Song of Songs*) of enlivening his text with the fiction of oral delivery.

Again, let no one think that this heavenly food, which is Christ, is like the food we consume in this world—for the food of souls is the glory of that vision of God. Yet it refreshes us and keeps us alive, so it is called food by analogy.

36. A spiritual vision of the virtue of loving obedience

After I had said the antiphon *Salve Regina* with the prayers that follow, and so forth, I added five Hail Marys as usual. In the meantime, as I recall, another heavenly revelation suddenly snatched me out of my bodily senses. It was like this. Impelled no doubt by the Holy Spirit, in a burst of the most passionate love I prayed to the Virgin Mary, the glorious mother who gave birth to God. I asked her by virtue of her loving obedience to approach God for me and pray that I would come to him, just as he promised me. At once, as it seemed to me, the simple maiden departed. She was most obedient, most humble and prompt, most eager to fulfill her task, and most sober in her purpose, free from all troubled thoughts. Without delay, in the twinkling of an eye,[103] she most lovingly delivered her message as she stood before the beloved Beloved.

At once I said to the Virgin what Samson's wife once said, or rather did. "Shed tears in his presence," I said, "even at his feet. But it is not for you to say, 'You hate me. You don't really love me, and that is why you don't want to explain the riddle you posed for the sons of my people.'[104] Still, you must bother him until he tells you the day of my death.[105] And then you must tell me, although your affection could not delay, because I languish so

103. 1 Cor 15:52.

104. Judg 14:16.

105. Despite the resolution of his debate with Christ, Methley shows that he still longs to die as soon as possible. God continued to resist his prayer, for he was 34 at the time of writing and lived to be 77. He died in 1527 or 1528, fortunately before the English Reformation.

fervently for love! But if he won't tell you, say to him what Delilah said to Samson. (I do not mean the harlot, but the woman who lived in the valley of Sorek.) She asked, 'How can you say you love me when your spirit is not with me?'[106] Scripture says of that woman that 'because she bothered him and clung to him constantly for many days, not giving him a moment of peace, his soul was exhausted and weary almost to death. Then he revealed the truth of the matter and told her the source of his strength.'[107] You too, gracious Virgin, never cease!"

That was the subject of my vision. Now, mother Mary, as I finish this book I promise you by God's grace that, as a reward for your loving obedience, I will recite the angelic greeting once every day, insofar as I can. But if I miss a day out of forgetfulness or real need, it will not be a sin. I here give thanks to God through you and entrust this book to the church. Praise and honor to God forever and ever! Amen.

Here ends *The Bedroom of the beloved Beloved*.

106. Judg 16:4; 16:15.
107. Judg 16:16-17. Medieval typology is often unexpected, but asking the Virgin Mary to imitate one of the most villainous women in Scripture may set a record for strangeness.

The Refectory of Salvation

**Here begins *The Refectory of Salvation*.
How those who abandon earthly things receive
a hundredfold even now, along with heavenly things.**

"Amen, I say to you: there is no one who abandons house or brothers or sisters or father or mother or children or lands for my sake and the sake of my name, who does not receive a hundredfold even now in this age—houses and brothers and sisters and mother and children and lands, with persecutions; and in the future age, eternal life."[1]

Because it is the Truth who promises, there is no doubt that he will keep his promise. But we must wait for what is promised and understand what he said devoutly. How then do we receive a hundredfold, even now in this age? He means that whoever clings to God is one spirit with him,[2] so that the Lord is his possession. Through love, therefore, he comes to possess not only creation but even the Creator. That is why I abandoned all earthly things, and I obtained all heavenly things together with earthly ones. Now indeed I possess them in hope, but hereafter in reality. Because there is no comparison between the finite (that which has an end) and the infinite (that which has no end), clearly those who abandon all present things "for my sake and the sake of my name" not only receive a hundredfold, even now in this age, but infinitely more.

1. Mark 10:29-30.
2. 1 Cor 6:17.

What does it mean to abandon all things if not to reject carnal affection for what is superficial, that is, for outward appearances? Thus, living by grace in a hermitage, I am writing *The Refectory of Salvation* for you. Once you know what the heavenly feasts are like, you will desire to be refreshed with heavenly food and run thirstily toward God at all times in holy desire. The better to achieve this goal, let us first proclaim the angelic greeting and seek grace through the Mother of grace—the woman who found the grace that Eve lost.[3]

Hail Mary, full of grace, the Lord is with you; blessed [are you among women].[4]

1. On fulfilling the will of God voluntarily, and on drunken love

"I have eaten my honeycomb with my honey, I have drunk my wine with my milk."[5] Surely I have desired to be dissolved and be with Christ[6] because, as he well knows, I languish for his love[7]—not love of the world. Illumined in the spirit, I saw and affectively felt the will of God and the heavenly court, and all I could say was, Let the will of lovers be done! My will is mortified, therefore, and my affection is eager. I am ready to die at any moment, yet I am still delayed by God, whose will I have voluntarily tried to fulfill instead of my own. But love, full of desire and impatient of delay, rises up in its way like a violent drunk.[8] It adjures the Beloved for his own sake with the violence of love, commanding and rebuking him, saying: "Receive my spirit, for I languish for love!"[9]

---

3. The *Ave* of the prayer *Ave Maria* reverses the name of *Eva*.

4. Luke 1:28.

5. Song 5:1.

6. Phil 1:23.

7. Song 2:5; 5:8.

8. *Vt violentus immo vero vt vinolentus.* Cf. Song 5:1: "Eat, friends, and drink and be drunken (*inebriamini*), dearest ones."

9. Acts 7:58; Song 2:5.

Hence it is that today, in the year 1487 on the feast of the translation of Saint Hugh of Lincoln,[10] when I got up to say Prime in my cell at Mount Grace, suddenly angelic singing came upon me with holy song so that I could scarcely remain standing, physically unharmed, to finish Prime. But afterward, to say Terce of our Lady, I returned to the bed that I always have prepared for this purpose, throwing myself down on it at full length—and I almost lost command of my body. Or rather, I lost the power of speech like a person about to die, for love is strong as death.[11] And so I lay there crying, sighing, languishing, and groaning: "O who will tell the Beloved that I languish for love?"[12]

So indeed, I have learned from experience innumerable times, just as I did then, that David's words are true: "In a voice of exultation and confession, a sound of feasting."[13] Because of feasts like the one I enjoyed then with song and jubilation, I broke into these words for you to imitate: "I have eaten my honeycomb," etc.

2. On knowledge of truth obtained through the illumination of God

In a spiritual illumination, I saw a debate between two parties, and I was amazed that neither one understood the other. And look! I was illumined by the Spirit of God, who reveals the truth to anyone who is pleasing in his eyes. By no means can anyone know and defend the truth—except perhaps in ignorance, as a blind man may shoot a hare—unless he is illumined by the Spirit of God or else hears it from teachers through the faith of the church. Yet, as it is written, "no one knows whether he is worthy of hatred or love."[14] It is amazing how some people die for the truth even when

10. October 6.
11. Song 8:6.
12. Song 5:8.
13. Ps 41:5.
14. Eccl 9:1.

it is difficult to discern. Yet it is the Spirit that gives life; the flesh profits nothing.[15] Let no one presume to say who sees and who does not, unless he has a revelation from the Spirit of God. As for those who knowingly see, God has revealed the truth to them. Those who do not see are deceived when they imagine that they see. So I was astounded and afraid, and I said in wonder to a person who was sitting with me, "If you had seen what I saw, you would have been afraid all the days of your life."

Look! At once I saw two men. As for their consciences, I dare say that each of them would rather have been killed for the truth than lose the argument. They were arguing over words, and each one said with certainty that the truth was on his side. But neither one understood the other or knew which part of his account was true and which was false. Finally the merciful God enlightened both of their minds—and he showed that there was truth on both sides.

I have said these things to show you that no one can be refreshed with heavenly food (the chief subject of this book) if he is ensnared by questions of opinion and does not wish to yield himself wholly to peace. And if he is not illumined, he opens himself to the danger of falsehood.

3. On bodily observances in prayer

While I was intoxicated in devotion, in song, jubilation, and resounding harmony, I heard a voice of exultation and confession, a sound of feasting.[16] Following my usual custom, I was supposed to kiss an object, a bare post on my stall where the name of Jesus was written, while saying the words of a prayer. But I could not do this without difficulty, for the more peaceful the spirit is, the

---

15. John 6:64.

16. Ps 41:5. Methley's pet theme of *canor* is indebted to Richard Rolle. *Jubilus* or jubilation is a joyful song without words, often performed in mystical rapture. It need not be audible.

more devout it is. I chose therefore to pray and worship in spirit and in truth, for the Father seeks such worshipers,[17] and so does the Son. So I left off my previous observance, at least for that time.

If any scrupulous person claims that one should never do this, he can worship mentally in this way, using his imagination. Afterward he may come to jubilant song and learn that love is strong as death, and nothing that is desired can compare with it. For then, as I said before, he will lie sighing and shouting, rebuking and adjuring God himself for love's sake, in the most reverent way, begging to pass from this world to the fathers. For his song of charity is this: "I adjure you, sons of Jerusalem, if you find the Beloved, tell him that I languish for love."[18]

4. On spiritual shouting with poetic song and jubilation

On the day before the feast of Pope Saint Mark, the distinguished confessor,[19] I fell into a languor of love, wounded by charity.[20] I cried out in the most marvelous way in the spirit—not just in devotion, but in spiritual shouting with poetic song, sometimes with jubilation. But the Beloved, who is exceedingly kind, could not endure this or wait very long. So he came down from his royal throne and leapt into my spirit[21] with more ardent love, with perceptible joy of the heart, and said, "Here I am, for you called me."[22] And I remembered the Scripture that says, "Before you call on me, I will say, 'Here I am,' "[23] because his coming was so swift.

17. John 4:23.
18. Song 5:8. The Vulgate reads "daughters of Jerusalem." Sons (*filii* for *filie*) could be either a scribal error or a deliberate adaptation for a masculine audience.
19. This feast falls on October 7.
20. Song 4:9.
21. Wis 18:15.
22. 1 Sam 3:9.
23. Isa 58:9.

5. On firm faith in heavenly things, and on the future resurrection

While I was pondering that verse of Scripture, the word of the Lord came to me in a sudden inspiration. He said he would kindle me to more ardent love by asking a question—not that my heart in any way doubted. So he asked, "Do you have so much faith in Christ that you would dare to die and be with him?" It was as if he had said, "If the things they say about the future life are not true, you will be deceived and lose everything." When I had heard this, I desired much more fervently than before to be dissolved and be with Christ, for whose love I languish. And I said yes, I would dare to suffer death for the firm catholic faith.

6. On the dance of the heart

O wondrous exchange[24]—to sell the temporal and buy the eternal, to sell what is carnal and buy what is spiritual! Indeed, this is to sell what is mutable (by turning the mind away from worldly love) and buy what is immutable, that is, angelic contemplation and a dwelling in heaven, as the Apostle says: "Our way of life is in heaven."[25]

Today, that is, the day after the feast of Saint Dionysus, the great contemplative,[26] just after the eighth hour (according to the English way of reckoning the hours), I began to say Terce alone in choir,[27] with my bodily eyes closed and my spiritual eyes open.

---

24. *O admirabile commercium.* An antiphon for the Feast of the Circumcision (Use of York) reads, "O wondrous exchange! The Creator of humankind, taking body and soul, deigned to be born of the Virgin."

25. Phil 3:20.

26. The feast is October 9. This is Dionysus the Areopagite, aka Saint Denis, the great inspiration of apophatic mystics.

27. According to John Clark and James Hogg, this indicates that Methley held the office of sacristan at the time. Carthusian statutes indicate that the sacristan was never to leave his cell without permission except to sound the bell for the hours or say the Divine Office. He was always to perform the Office and the Hours of the Virgin in church, while other monks said them in their cells. But note that four days earlier (chap. 1), Methley was saying the Hours in his cell.

Then jubilant melody descended upon me with melodious jubilation, together with the amorous languor that can heal all things—and they have not yet departed from me. Rather, my heart is perceptibly dancing in my chest even as I write, and it is now after ten in the morning on the same day.

Perhaps you would like to hear about the state I was in during the celebration of Mass. But allow me first to cry out to him a little with surpassing exultation: I can die because love is strong as death, and surely, surely I languish for love! So my heart is still dancing in my chest, which is a great sign of the presence of the Beloved. O heart! Crushed and humbled[28] at first because of sin, deign now to be crushed by excessive love and break into a thousand fragments! Deign to burst[29] and leap up to the Beloved, or else you will continue to endure such great affliction as you remain confined in the body. But depart in freedom, and dwell from now on in the heart of him who opened his heart for you with a lance[30] of great gladness on the day of your wedding, the day of the gladness of his heart.[31] O Jesu Jesu Jesu! How long will you delay, and when will you cry, "Come, come, come and be crowned"?[32] This is the way my heart melted.[33] In fact, I almost faint and lose command of my body, for I am forced to stop writing, suspend my pen, and cry out, "O O O Jesu Jesu Jesu! How long will you delay, and when will you cry, "Come, come, come and be crowned"?

There is no vainglory in my mind—your Majesty is the witness—nor is my heart shaken by any pleasure from this experience. For my heart is almost completely torn apart and mangled because I languish for great love, even now as I write to you,

---

28. Ps 50:19.

29. *crepere. Marginal gloss: "Crepo*, that is, to break or shatter something by force. It can be used in the absolute sense, as in *Judas crepuit*, or in a mediated sense, as *to sowne, breke, or brest."*

30. Referring to the crucifixion; John 19:34.

31. Song 3:11.

32. Song 4:8.

33. Song 5:6.

dearest brothers. Nor does my peace ever leave me, but as long as I am awake, my heart is absolutely always at peace.[34] At least I have peace on my own part, though not from the devil, who scarcely ever stops tempting me. But I pay no attention to him, and thus I have peace, as it is written: "My eyes are always on the Lord, for he will release my feet from the snare."[35]

7. On an incident involving a struggle with death

So the good Lord, whose mercy endures forever,[36] dwells with me just as he once did with Samuel. Giving me strength, he aroused my heart to much more fervent love while I was hearing Mass than when I was saying Terce. Compelled by the increase of charity, I began to cry out, "How long will I cry and how long will I endure?"[37] and "Would that I could leave the dwelling of this exile!" Who knows how often I repeated these and similar words? O fiery, impetuous river that streams from my mouth and envelops me in fire, when will you make an end of me? For the healing sickness, the outbursts of sudden joy, the lyrical song— these never depart from me. Rather, the very sweetness of devotion, along with the ceaseless dance in my heart and the ineffable, inconceivable joy, bring my life into bitterness until the Beloved whom I love is bestowed on me, until the day dawns when God will give not just delicious delicacies, but his very self in everlasting salvation. For the spiritual savor that I sense comes not from this unclean world, but from God.[38]

---

34. This might seem like a contradiction: how could Methley's heart be at once "torn apart and mangled," yet "always at peace"? He doubtless means that even if his peace is troubled by the languor of love, it never yields to earthly cares or temptations.

35. Ps 24:15.

36. Ps 117:1-4.

37. Hab 1:2.

38. Another passage of Rollean alliteration.

I had intended to continue my narrative, but the bell for the Hours of the day and those of our Lady Saint Mary had sounded, so I ceased at once. Yet I could not remain standing while I said them, for the joyful languor that filled me made me incapable of such bodily observances and compelled me to utter the digressions I have inserted here. But now I will bring to light what I have deferred.

As I was hearing Mass, I fainted and lost command of my body. With a most impetuous impulse of love, I begged God to take my spirit. Suddenly, as I was touched by his hand and urged by his spirit, I was compelled unexpectedly to say, "See, I am ready!"[39] Because of the way my heart was dancing, I thought it wanted to leap out through my mouth, and in this way I would give up my spirit.[40] Thus, as I sighed from the depth of my heart, groaning and weeping, I was again suddenly touched by the hand of God in the spirit. Caught between the actual pressure of death and the remembrance of my departure, again I thought that my spirit would depart at once. So I agonized for almost two hours, while my body was greatly weakened and afflicted by the cold. Yet my loving state of mind did not recede.

See the kind of feast I offer you here in this *Refectory of Salvation!* Eat rich foods and drink much sweet wine, and send portions to each other for those who have prepared none for themselves,[41] so that God may be praised in his gifts and blessed for all his benefits when everyone has doubled his talent.[42] That is, let one tell his story to another, let one write to another, or give of his abundance or proclaim it. For I have eaten my honeycomb with my honey, I have drunk my wine with my milk.[43] And God is my

---

39. 2 Cor 12:14.

40. Cf. Matt 27:50.

41. Neh 8:10; used as an antiphon for communion.

42. Cf. Matt 25:14-30. Methley indicates that he saw the sharing of mystical experiences as an act of charity.

43. Song 5:1.

witness that I am not moved to vainglory, but my heart is always at peace—thanks to him forever and ever.

8. On desire and anticipation, and on the remembrance of death and the passion of Christ

O bitter death and passion of Christ! Grant me to depart from this mortal body, for life is bitter to me as long as I live because I languish for surpassing love. Scarcely anyone could believe how great this bitterness is, or understand what it is like, unless he had experienced it. For such a person feels no pain but has joy and great glory before the whole heavenly court, as Scripture affirms in the book of Wisdom: "her companionship has no bitterness, nor her company tedium, but joy and gladness."[44] Even so, I cried out mightily in spirit, "O bitter death and passion of Christ! Grant me to depart from this mortal body," and so forth. I reached this point through desire and anticipation, urged by pure affection, when I cried out, "Who will tell the Beloved that I languish for love?"[45] As I think how many times I have waited for our Lord and our Lady Saint Mary, who long ago promised me eternal life, an idea has occurred to me: What if [my] hour has already come, suddenly and unexpectedly? If the languor of my desire had grown the way it began, that would surely have been the hour of my death, for by merely remembering it, I seemed almost to give up my spirit.

9. How the impulse of love arouses the spirit to seek what God wills

On the feast of Saint Wilfred, the day before the translation of Saint Edward the King and Confessor,[46] when I was beginning to

---

44. Wis 8:16.

45. Song 5:8.

46. Saint Wilfred's feast is October 12; Saint Edward the Confessor's is October 13.

say Prime for Friday with the psalm, "Hear my judgment, O Lord, give heed to my prayer,"[47] and so forth, I was suddenly rapt into ecstasy in the twinkling of an eye.[48] By the arousal of my spirit I recognized the messenger of love, and my heart was touched by the question of my bodily death or dissolution. Because of a movement in my spirit, I felt that I should respond to the urging of love, so I asked, "What do you wish, my Beloved? And what about *my* wishes, Beloved?" He asked me whether I would be prepared in my will to die. I answered this question with a sudden inspiration: as matters stood, I was ready to die with the melting of my soul, and I surely grew faint with great love.

10. On the rapture of love in ecstasy, with the melting of the heart

Later on the same day, at the same time and place, while I was saying Terce of blessed Mary, I was suddenly ravished again with a perceptible touching of my heart. Dissolved in tears, I felt my heart melting like wax before the fire,[49] though I think its substance remained intact. But in its own way, it tasted like honey in its love, as if it had melted into honey. And I marveled at the vision, even though I had experienced it very often. How could I be ravished so suddenly, in the twinkling of an eye, when I had been utterly unaware before? At once a voice came to me—not a voice at that time, but another kind of inspiration about this matter.[50] If it were uttered with the tongue, it would require no little time to expound. And I marveled at how suddenly the spirit can be ravished into ecstasy.

---

47. Ps 16:1.

48. Cf. 2 Cor 12:2; 1 Cor 15:52; 2 Cor 5:13.

49. Ps 21:15.

50. This sentence is incoherent and may be corrupt. Another possibility is that Methley is conflating the "voice" he heard on this occasion with a similar inspiration at another time.

11. On ecstasy and frequent raptures in languishing love

On the day before the feast of Saints Crispin and Crispinian,[51] I had risen to say Prime of the day. As the devil is always devising some new temptation against me, so he did then. I don't know how many new temptations he has devised to make my mind offer the first fruits of its love to the world instead of God. But far be it from me—even if he still has many temptations in store for me. Often he brings four, five, or even six new temptations to see if I will find the delight of my heart in any of them. But as I call on the name of Jesus without disdain or lukewarmness, at once I repel and cast out all these temptations—and I languish for love.

Very often I feel perceptible love in my heart, so I am unexpectedly lifted on high by excessive love. This excess is above reason, not beneath it. Then I adjure God with an impulse of the most languishing love: "I adjure you by your bitter death, insofar as it pleases you, let me die! For I languish for love." There is no more delay in the spiritual utterance of these words than in the ecstasy itself. It occurs in the twinkling of an eye, with no prior deliberation or knowledge. Sometimes, though, I utter these or similar words in the sheer affection of love, but without full rapture, as if I had grown used to them. As I suddenly fall to the ground on my knees in prayer, the remembrance of death is very pleasing to me, for I languish for love. Often, while rapt in an ecstasy of love or suddenly impelled by loving affection to utter these words, I have almost fainted—I do not know how many times. But it has been very often, even though I might be arranging the house, the bed, the windows, or the doors as I usually do, and lifting up my hands with continual prayer and invocation of the name of Jesus.

When I had reached my stall, I could not speak for a while, for I had too recently grown faint with love. But then, O how frequent were the raptures of love! My soul melted as the Beloved spoke,[52]

---

51. This feast is October 25.
52. Song 5:6.

and I sighed, adjured him, and cried out, "Love, love, love!" And
I spoke many words of love. But the devil, seeing that he had
gained nothing, made a mighty effort to call my mind away from
contemplation. For he attacked my mind to make me think diligently, so that I would cease my words in order to write them
down later.[53] He did not obtain what he wanted, for I preferred
to forget them all rather than be drawn away from contemplation,
even if I had received a revelation for someone about a special
case related to some need—words to be repeated or recorded.
These things I never remember, [or] I forget some part of them,
for the effect [of the devil's attack] was to make me forget.

Yet I remember this, which is a fruit of salvation. As I have
been so frequently rapt into ecstasy in the twinkling of an eye,
with the exaltation of my mind and the touch of God's loving
hand, at every moment I am asked if I wish to die because I languish for love. Suddenly I replied to the Savior as Peter once did,
"Lord, you know everything; you know that I desire to be dissolved, for I languish for love."[54] Thanks be to you, Lord!

12. On the Mass

As I celebrated Mass that day, let me say that I was consumed by
sighs and wounds of love. When it came time for me to receive
the Eucharist, I said to the Beloved that even though he was now
present, he gave me no answer, not a single word. Then all at once
he said, "I am right here in the affection of love." For in the twinkling of an eye, I felt a perceptible languor of love in my mind.
This made me so faint that I could by no means continue until I
had recovered my spirit. But first I rested my head on my elbow

---

53. This textually corrupt passage has been corrected, but remains incoherent. The
editors suggest a probable meaning: "The devil wanted to distract Methley from his
acts of love for God by making him think, with a view to writing them down, but
failed in this." *The Works of Richard Methley*, p. 104.

54. John 21:17; Phil 1:23; Song 2:5.

because of the delights of love. Then, returning to the Eucharist, I related to the Beloved the words or rather the wounds of my heart, for I had grown faint with love. When I had finished Mass, I fainted again and again, having become utterly languid. For my life consists of love, languor, sweetness, warmth, and song,[55] yet perceptible warmth is the rarest. The Beloved has promised me that I would experience love more often in languor, just as the kindly Richard of Hampole experienced it more often in warmth. I have not read that he experienced such frequent languor.

13. On the sheep of Saint Peter the Apostle

I recall that sometimes, while praying at the canon of the Mass and certainly at other times, as I melted with love, I would invoke the apostle Peter. I busied myself to implore his aid, knowing that I had once been entrusted to him by Christ through his successors. Remembering that Christ had said, "Feed my sheep,"[56] I accused Peter out of excessive love, which knows no reason. Because he delayed to transfer me to the Beloved with the help of his prayers, I said he was bound at least to take care of me, not just from natural affection but as my pastor. I accused him, so to speak, by saying, "At least acknowledge and help a sheep under your care, as Christ entrusted me to you when he said 'Feed my sheep.'"

14. On reproaching God through excess of love

It is no wonder that I affectionately reproached the apostle Peter, for I often reproached God himself in a wondrous way, beyond reason, for keeping me apart from him for so long. (Yet in another way, he is not absent from me in the hermitage.) Thinking about

---

55. *Nam vita mea consistit in amore, languore, dulcore, feruore, canore.* This is Methley's most explicit acknowledgement of his debt to Richard Rolle, the hermit of Hampole.

56. John 21:17.

death, as people call it,[57] I reproached him with a divine prohibition that he should by no means keep me apart from him after death. Many are the loving conversations of this kind between affectionate lovers! But since there is nothing better than chaste love, I pursue that alone above all other gifts—the good kind of love that desires, possesses, and embraces the Beloved for himself alone, not for the sake of anything else. The Beloved never allows any failure to occur on his part, nor does he ever grow weary of showing affection, no matter how often. Rather, the more frequent it is, the sweeter it is—though also the rarer it is, the more precious it is. This indeed is marvelous to say and beyond human custom, that anything should be sweeter because it is more frequent, yet also more precious because it is rarer. But what I have just said is a difference between the pleasures of divine love and human love.

15. That all earthly goods are vain compared with heavenly sweetness

After the feast of the apostles Simon and Jude, that is, on the day before the vigil of All Saints,[58] at the Vespers of our Lady Saint Mary, the glorious Virgin Mother of God, I was saying this psalm, "I was glad when they said to me, we will go to the house of the Lord."[59] Suddenly and unexpectedly, a languor of love came upon me, with the surpassingly sweet delights that the soul enjoys in union with the Beloved. I fainted, unable to bear his weight because of my soul's languor. And I burst out in a spiritual voice and exclaimed with all my heart, yearning to be dissolved and be with the Beloved, for whose love I grew violently faint: "Vanity of vanities,

---

57. *vt vulgariter dicitur.* What the vulgar call "death" is, for Methley, eternal life and union with the Beloved.

58. The feast of Saints Simon and Jude is October 28; the Vigil of All Saints (Halloween) is October 31. Thus this experience took place on October 30.

59. Ps 121:1.

all is vanity!"[60] It seemed to me that no creature could know how great the languor of love is, or imagine the immense pain of the languishing soul, except one to whom this experience is given. So in my spirit I summoned all creatures to lament with me and grieve over me because of my extreme pain. "Come and mourn over me, all you creatures," I said, "for my pain knows no bounds as I contemplate this truth: 'Vanity of vanities, all is vanity.'"

The initial cause of this thought was as follows. To improve my cell, I had had the wall broken to put in a window, admitting wholesome air and making it a brighter place to write. For some reason—I don't know why—it was not yet finished. I'm not sure if God is testing and proving me to see if I am perfectly mortified, like a pilgrim, or if the devil won't let it be finished so I will be bothered for a longer time. One thing I know: by the grace of the Beloved, my heart is at peace. But since the noise of the workers is bothersome, especially because this work is being done in my study, I do not write now. Yet my mind is unquiet and impatient because of the celestial postponement; the vision of the Beloved and his kingdom is delayed. This is what compels me to cry, "Vanity of vanities, all is vanity."

16. How a Carthusian said the Placebo *on All Saints' Day*

After Vespers on All Saints' Day,[61] the superior of the community, in the lord prior's absence, required me out of charity to take a little supper in my cell after [reading in] the refectory.[62] But first I came up to say the customary prayers and the *Placebo* according to the rule of the order.[63] Clarifying my intention first, as I always

---

60. Eccl 1:2.

61. November 1.

62. Methley was the assigned reader for the week. After reading during the meal in the refectory, the reader could take supper privately in his cell.

63. *Placebo* is the antiphon for Vespers in the Office of the Dead, said on All Souls' Day (November 2) and many other occasions.

do, I began to think how eagerly people ask the Carthusians to pray for them and the souls of their dear ones out of charity, because of the holiness of the order—though they surely know little of it. Indeed, all who have no experience in this order would say, if they were to experience it, what the Queen of Sheba once said to Solomon: "Your virtues have surpassed your reputation!" [64]

So in the simplicity of my heart, ascribing nothing to myself (for all good things come from God), I began to say the *Placebo* for all the faithful departed. My intention was that God should receive this prayer in the best way he knew, because the holy intention with which a Carthusian should say it surpassed my meager ability. In a brief moment, just as I was thinking this thought, suddenly there came upon me a languor of love that made me lose command of my body. All of a sudden I mentally cried out, "Honor and power and strength be to our God forever and ever, Amen!" [65] It was as if I had said, "Lord, not mine but yours be the praise and honor [66] that I am a Carthusian. You know explicitly, in every detail, what I intend implicitly in this prayer for all the faithful. My intention has no limits, for I intend to pray in every good way, far beyond what I or any mortal can know or imagine." [67]

17. On natural and spiritual joy

As I was thinking about these things a little later, again there came upon me that perceptible love and languor that transcends all the senses. Here I am speaking to all Christians: whenever it comes with violence, it ravishes the mind above the bodily senses. So as that glorious sensation came upon me, I saw mentally and spiritually, or rather I experienced in an almost physical way, that my joy had no bounds, reaching all the way to God. And I said to him,

64. 2 Chr 9:6.
65. Rev 7:12.
66. Cf. Ps 113b:1.
67. Cf. Eph 3:20.

"My food is to be lifted up to you in a natural and spiritual way,[68] and to ascribe all the good that I have to you, who bestowed it on me." Indeed, I felt myself naturally moved and experienced joy beyond measure in this: that I should praise him, not myself, and enjoy him, not his creatures or his gifts, as if they had come from me and not from him. So I often repeated these words: "My food is to ascribe all the good things in my life to you." Anyone who lives otherwise behaves unnaturally, and anyone who lives this way has full and natural joy. This alone is enough for him. Delight in a creature never says "enough,"[69] but is always wandering from one thing to another, hungry and thirsty. It can never be satisfied, for it is impossible for human nature to find complete joy in creatures.

18. On the desire for death

On All Souls' Day I rose and began to say Prime, as I do every day.[70] While I get dressed, I say a certain prayer mentioning the day I entered the order, with the intention that my spirit might always be as eager as on the first day. But I have continued saying this prayer so long that I have conceived a desire to think about my departure rather than my entrance. Hence, suddenly touched in spirit with the most languishing love, I yearned to give up my spirit in that very moment, with no further delay. Because I began by thinking at dawn every day about my entrance into the order, I am now compelled to think about my departure, that is, my bodily death. Or rather, in a moment of rapture, I am driven to give up my spirit instead of merely thinking about it. But either way, it is through Christ, as he said: "If anyone enters through me, he will go in and out and find pasture."[71]

68. Cf. John 4:34.
69. Cf. Prov 30:15-16.
70. November 2.
71. John 10:9.

19. What a true contemplative's state of mind should be

I have a certain prayer that I say every day, remembering how the glorious Mary Magdalene chose the best part, which will not be taken away from her.[72] Early on the morning of All Souls' Day, when I had come to that part of the prayer, I was making my bed as usual. Suddenly a rapture of the most languishing love came upon me and forced me to sit down, my mind suspended in heaven. So I stopped what I was doing until I had recovered my spirit enough to continue. When I finally reached my stall to say Prime of the day, having finished my voluntary prayers, I did have my mind on the meaning of the prayers. But through the suggestion of the enemy or mere flightiness, I also had some other thoughts mingled with these. They were not evil, but good and holy in themselves; yet they were inappropriate for that time, for it was not profitable to think about such things then.

And lo! Suddenly a languor ravished me into perceptible sweetness of devotion and made me think of my desire for death. At once I understood that my previous thoughts had been vain. Or rather, if one's state of mind must vacillate, it is better to think about death than anything else. Gradually proceeding with Prime, I was very sweetly brought back to peace of mind, like someone in Saint Noah's ark during the Flood. As I was kneeling afterward to say the prayers of Prime for the day, once again that sweetest languor came upon me. When one is speaking from sheer affection, the most restful position is not standing but sitting or kneeling, resting the head on the elbows. And I was amazed to find that there were tears on my cheeks, because in that peaceful state I had been unaware of them; I was not paying attention to them or thinking about them. But I state this to the praise of God: sometimes the mere thought of Christ's coming, or bodily death, or the name of Jesus when I call upon him, brings a perceptible,

72. Luke 10:42. Medieval tradition identified Mary Magdalene with Mary of Bethany, the sister of Martha.

languishing sweetness upon me. I also experience outbursts of joyous song very often—night and day without ceasing.

See how I have received a hundredfold from the Savior in this world! And I hope to have eternal life in the future age,[73] through the mercy of him for whose love I languish (thanks to him) so vehemently, so frequently, and so recently.

20. *What kind of grace can be earned by giving alms*

After Vespers on the feast of Saint Leonard the abbot,[74] I gave myself over to peaceful devotion as usual. It occurred to me that I had once visited an elderly recluse, who lived in a little cell next to a chapel dedicated to God and Saint Leonard. She had been ill for seven years or more, as I remember, and could not leave her bed. Her hands were so withered that she could not even lift them to her mouth. I secretly gave her serving woman substantial alms, but in public I gave small alms, like the others who were with me, and I asked her not to publicize my action.[75] But she did not honor my wish. Instead, soon after she left me, she made it known to everyone. Some praised me and others blamed me, saying I never wished to prosper. A few days afterward the recluse died.

As for me, I obtained so much grace from this act that within three months, I too was led to a solitary cell to live there as a Carthusian. Every year when the feast of Saint Leonard comes around, I always feel special devotion when I remember this act, and after God I am especially devoted to the memory of this saint, since it occurred on his feast day.

I am afflicted with such profound ennui from the desire to see Christ, for whose love I so often languish, that I find it burdensome to see any creature. If I could—with all due respect for the order, the priesthood, and this bodily life—I would wish never to see

---

73. Mark 10:30.

74. November 6.

75. This detail suggests that before he entered the hermitage, Methley had been a person of means.

any creature again until I see Christ, if I could only find a suitable place to stay.[76]

21. On spiritual song in the mind, which is to be desired above all music

On the feast of the Holy Relics,[77] I rose as usual to sing Prime of the day in church. This feast is a very solemn one among the Carthusians, although many are unaware of the reason for it. It falls on the day before the feast of Saint Theodore the Martyr, who was burned by a tyrant for the love of Christ. So when I had risen and meditated as usual on my entrance into the order and my departure (that is, the day of my death), suddenly an ecstatic sensation came upon me, full of melody and celestial harmony. No small sweetness and glory are given with the name of Jesus! As my mind was exalted in ecstasy, I shrank from the memory of both my entrance and my departure. In the experience of this song and heavenly music, I cared little for (though I do not say I despised) any other songs, joys, and meditations whatsoever— whether the eagerness of my entrance into the order or the joyful thought of my departure. And rightly so! For this is the fruition; the rest is laborious exercise. This heavenly music is the thing itself, not just a thought or meditation about it. So I rightly cared little for anything except this one thing, by the grace of the Beloved and the ecstatic sensation that I had.

22. On spiritual slumber and a feeling of dying, in spite of bodily affliction

On the feast of Saint Bricius the bishop,[78] when I rose to say Prime in my cell, I wanted to admit no thought, whether good or evil.

---

76. Methley identifies with the recluse, who attained a solitude even greater than his own as a Carthusian.

77. A special Carthusian observance on November 8.

78. November 13.

Instead, as I usually did, I pursued song and jubilation by invoking the name of Jesus over and over. And look what happened! Though the bitter cold afflicted my tender body, my mind grew drunk on the sweetest melody. Singing in its gladness, it slept in utter peace in its way, as if riding the waves of the Flood in Noah's ark. The inclement chill pierced right through my sides, yet I found meditating on death to be the sweetest thought, accompanied by a perceptible feeling of dying. Because of its vehemence, I did not want to take any thought for the cold or anything else. Instead I lay or sat there, or else knelt and rested my head on my elbow and hands—singing, languishing, slumbering. I rested like this for a whole hour, for that sensation was so joyful that I could sustain this melody, savor, and slumber[79] with no great mental difficulty, despite the cold. Yet I was bound to fulfill the bodily observance of the order at least in part, if not in full. But when a violent impulse or any ecstatic sensation comes on, surpassing other things, I think it best to abandon everything for awhile and yield to Christ's teaching and control. "All who are led by the Spirit of God are children of God."[80]

23. On the celebration of Mass with impetuous affection, above reason

Two days before the feast of Saint Edmund of Pontigny, the archbishop of Canterbury and primate of England,[81] as I was approaching the steps of the altar to say the Lord's Prayer before Mass in the Carthusian manner, an ecstatic sensation suddenly came upon me. Passing into an ecstasy beyond reason, I adjured the Beloved. I adjured him, I say—but without the use of reason—that with his holy call, he would deign to snatch me out of the

---

79. *saporem soporemque.* Perhaps alternate readings, though Methley could have intended the wordplay.

80. Rom 8:14.

81. The feast falls on November 16.

worldly abode of this body. Since I had prayed to him with tears so often and in so many ways before, yet had not been heard, my intention was that at least this time, through the efficacy of that Mass, he might delay me no longer. Even so, he has delayed me until the present day. Would that even now he would hearken—he whose ears heed the prayers of lovers[82]—and just once say "Come!"[83]

These things took place on Wednesday before the feast of Saint Edmund. In the present year, 1487, that feast fell on a Friday.

24. On a new course in the spiritual feast

On the following Thursday, the day before the archbishop's feast, when I had risen as usual to say Prime of the day—as always, rejecting all thoughts except the actual, present embrace of the Beloved—I came to my stall and began the service of God. Now, even though the love of God should be always fresh and never weary, the Beloved visited me in a new way, different from the slumber I described on Saint Bricius's day. For I spent that whole hour in delights, enjoying impetuous affection with jubilant song and melody, mingled with exultation, in great gladness of mind. It should be well known to everyone, lovers of God and the world alike, that for the love of God no time is more fitting than dawn and evening on any day you like. Wicked love of the world should never be allowed on any day, in any hour or minute. Yet at those times it is especially fitting for the conscience to gaze upon God.

25. On the feast of Saint Edmund, archbishop of Canterbury

On the feast of Saint Edmund the Archbishop in the aforesaid year, as I was sitting in my stall in my cell at Mount Grace, attending to my usual prayers, the Savior's grace visited me in this way. In the

82. Cf. Ps 33:16.
83. Rev 22:17.

twinkling of an eye, I was asked in spirit whether or not I wanted
to be with Christ in that sensation. As I answered in an instant,[84]
without delay, I felt myself suddenly translated through the air
somehow, leaving the whole visible world behind with all it contains. Although my body was in the world, my mind was in heaven,
and I felt certain sensations as if I were putting off my body—already fulfilling what will happen in the future at my bodily death.
A little afterward, as I proceeded with my prayers, once again I
was suddenly raised up in the twinkling of an eye, with the same
sensation of dying. From this you may truly know that through
grace, I have been enabled to give up my spirit habitually at the
first movement,[85] in some way, in order to be with the Beloved.

Even though I have not fully died, I have almost died on many
occasions. If my spirit has not departed, it has very often been on
the point of departure. But afterward even this sensation passed,
and again my spirit was suddenly caught up in ecstasy with the
most violent impulse, so that I could say nothing but "Jesu Jesu
Jesu! Jesu Jesu Jesu! Jesu Jesu Jesu!" After this, through the malice of the enemy, I began to think a few other good thoughts, which
however were not directed to the immediate presence of God.
Then the ecstatic sensation suddenly touched my mind again, in
an instant, and I could say nothing but "My beloved! My beloved!"
I repeated this many, many times.

26. On another new course in the spiritual feast

On the feast of Saint Hugh of Lincoln,[86] as I was approaching the
steps of the altar to say the Lord's Prayer before Mass, that adjura-

---

84. *In puncto*, a keyword of this section. Reminiscent of *The Cloud of Unknowing*
(chap. 4) with its focus on the smallest possible unit of time, and Julian of Norwich's
assertion that "I saw God in a poynte" (*A Revelation of Love*, chap. 11).

85. *In motu primo*. Preparation for death was a traditional goal of the monastic
life, but Methley understands his ecstasies as a special way of preparing for the death
he so urgently desires. The first hint of ecstasy is an occasion to assent to dying,
leaving the body behind "to be with the Beloved."

86. November 17.

tion of the Beloved that I spoke of before came upon me in a new way, with a new sensation. After Mass, not without the languor of love and peace (I do not say "of the Peacemaker," although he could be called that; but I say "of peace")—so I continued until the end of Mass.[87] After dining at table in the refectory with my brothers (in the literal sense), I came to my cell and another sensation came upon me, in yet another new way. I was enabled to sing in mind and body, in melody and jubilation with very great joy, as if I had entered into the Lord's Paradise. In this way I exulted, I say, through the grace of Jesus Christ the Beloved.

27. *What the letters in the name of Jesus signify*

On the day after the feast of Saint Hugh, when I had assisted the priest and arranged the corporals needed for the altar, reverently folding them,[88] I was suddenly illumined in spirit and understood the meaning of the last three letters in the name of Jesus, that is, SVS.[89] According to the ancients, S signified the number seven, but in modern times it also represents five. Then I saw that the letter S signifies the present life, which unfolds through the seven days of the week, always repeating from the first day. The letter V signifies the five senses, and because the V has two sides, it denotes both the inner and the outer senses. In this way its meaning is doubled. Because the V is closed at the bottom and open at the top, it means that a lover of Christ should close his outer and inner senses to vanities below while keeping his heart open to God above. He should do this not just for a little while, but always, as the letter signifies the whole present age. If he does this rightly in his way, his mind will be at rest with God like the saints in heaven, whom the Spirit has already told to rest from

---

87. *placoris, non dico placatoris, quamquam et hoc sustinui posset, sed placoris, dico.* The wordplay is hard to capture and the sentence is not grammatical.

88. Methley was serving as sacristan at this time.

89. The letters U and V are interchangeable in Latin. V is the Roman numeral for 5.

their labors.[90] This is indicated by the letter S in the third place, for the seventh age of the world—the age of rest for the blessed saints—is fittingly denoted by the letter S when it signifies seven. It is part of the mystery that this form of the number seven is rarely used, for there are very few people like this. Ah, so few! No one can easily imagine this, for the whole world is in the power of the evil one.[91] Yet until the end of the world some will be chosen, for even if the charity of many grows cold,[92] yet many are called, though few are chosen.[93] So says Christ, the searcher of hearts, who rewards and punishes morals.[94]

28. On the vanity of all creation, and on the virtue of synderesis[95]

On the feast of Saint Edmund, the glorious king and martyr of the English,[96] I was standing at first Vespers in choir with my brothers, singing the hymn *Ave maris stella*,[97] for it was the vigil of the Presentation of the glorious Virgin Mary, the Mother of God. That feast is observed on the day of Saint Columban the abbot.[98] As I was singing, I happened to think of the window I had caused

90. Rev 14:13.

91. 1 John 5:19.

92. Matt 24:12.

93. Matt 20:16; 22:14.

94. *scrutator cordium et retributor morum.* Cf. Rev 2:23.

95. According to the *Internet Encyclopedia of Philosophy, synderesis* is closely related to *conscience,* as "the innate principle in the moral consciousness of every person which directs the agent to good and restrains him from evil." But Methley probably alludes to a more mystical sense developed by Thomas Gallus in the prologue to his *Commentary on Isaiah.* There the *scintilla* (spark) of synderesis is the highest affective part of the soul, through which it is united to God. Gallus links it with the seraphim.

96. November 20.

97. "Hail, star of the sea," a well-known Marian hymn.

98. Both feasts fall on November 21. As the greater solemnity, the Presentation has both a first and a second Vespers.

to be made in the study where I write, to let in more light and air.[99] While this thought flitted briefly through my mind, I considered how one need follows another, for something I had thought finished had not lasted. Suddenly I felt great weariness as I longed for a sight of Christ, and I grew faint with perceptible love of him. Illumined in spirit while my soul melted, I broke out in this cry: "Vanity of vanities, all is vanity!"[100] And I was weary of my life, seeing that everything under the sun is vanity and nothing endures without change. Therefore my heart melted and tears welled up in my eyes.

But the spark of synderesis reminded me always to lift up my heart to God.[101] Doing this frequently recalled to my mind what I said before: "Vanity of vanities, all is vanity." After a little while, my soul melted again and I dissolved in sighs, and the spark of synderesis always reminded me to lift up my heart. So I would ask it, "Synderesis, what are you doing? What do you want with me, goading me like this? Don't you see that my mind finds no rest in any created being? Don't you see that I am weary of my life for the sake of seeing Christ? And I see in the spirit that compared with him, everything in the world is vanity. Yes, vanity of vanities!"

29. On falling asleep in the midst of the sea, lulled by the intoxication of love

What a wondrous exchange![102] In return for vile temporal things, freely given up for the Savior, we receive spiritual goods a hundredfold in this world and eternal life in the world to come.[103] On

---

99. See chap. 15 above.

100. Eccl 1:2.

101. *sursum cor habere ad deum*. Methley alludes to the dialogue preceding the eucharistic prayer.

102. *O admirabile commercium*, antiphon for the feast of the Circumcision.

103. See chap. 6 above.

the feast of Saint Cecilia the martyr,[104] I had risen from my writing to say the twelve psalms—that is, one nocturn of the Psalter—that I usually say before Vespers while walking outdoors. Suddenly there came upon me an impulse of soporific love that made me fall asleep in the spirit, ineffably plunged in a wondrous sea, drunk on the wine of spiritual intoxication.[105] In the same impulse I spiritually ran a vigorous race, directing the impulse of my spirit toward infinity. Yet I could not move a single part of my body without difficulty. So, unable to walk, I fell into my stall and did not rise until I had completed the twelve psalms or even more. I had grown drunk on wine from the most precious goblet—not from the tavern, no, but from the cavern of Christ's side. During this slumber and this race, as I exercised in the midst of the sea, I seemed to lie most peacefully amid crashing waves while the whole world shook around me. I do not think anyone who has not experienced this can know what it is like. For I felt as if I were lying in a deep, deep bath or a vat of wine, so thoroughly drunk I was!

30. On the antiphon Salve Regina, *on the prison of this world, and on mental music*

On the vigil of Saint Andrew,[106] I had risen for Matins as usual. After directing my mind to heaven with the name of Jesus by the appropriate use of reason, I began as usual to say the antiphon *Salve Regina*, honoring the Mother of mercy.[107] I renewed my intention that in this glorious Virgin's hands, anything that is un-

---

104. November 22.

105. Cf. Song 5:1.

106. The feast falls on November 30.

107. The Marian antiphon sung at the end of Compline from Trinity Sunday through Saint Andrew's day (the beginning of Advent): "Hail, O Queen, mother of mercy; hail, our life, our sweetness, and our hope. To thee we cry, to thee we sigh, groaning and weeping in this vale of tears. O our advocate, turn those thy merciful eyes toward us, and after this our exile, show unto us Jesus, the blessed fruit of thy womb. O merciful, O kind, O sweet Virgin Mary."

worthy in mortals might become acceptable to God. This intention was not only for me, but for all the faithful. Suddenly there came upon me a spiritual sensation of being in deep darkness, in a shadowy prison, bewailing the exile that we suffer here because Adam with his offspring was expelled from Paradise. By divine illumination I saw that everything in the world is vanity of vanities, compared with the true felicity that is in heaven. And I understood that this should be the exercise of all people, especially monks.

Afterward I remembered what I had seen in this illumination. Finally, as I was hurrying to Compline that night, I held the joy of heaven in my mind. Again I was illumined and beheld the eternal glory—never-ending, ineffable, inconceivable! This glory shall be given to all who meditate on the exile of Adam's children, count everything under the sun as vanity of vanities, and prefer to give themselves prayerfully, with all their hearts, to the love of God instead of the world. So I sang all night long with my spiritual mind until I hurried to bed and yielded to sleep—only to rise again for Matins. Thanks be to him who gave me this gift, with all the others, forever and ever.

31. On the terror of the devil who, incited by his own malice, envies the divine lover

The ancient enemy saw that he had gained nothing by his wicked wiles and, taking it badly, changed his method of temptation. So I rose for Matins and put on our habit, saying a prayer as usual. As soon as I had put on the cowl, some spirit or other came up from behind and pushed me on the shoulder so hard that I almost fell. His touch was perceptible! I quivered with fear at the first movement, but then I thought that no mortal was with me in the cell at this hour of the night, so I realized it was a spirit who wanted to frighten me. After I had fortified myself with the sign of the cross and written the words "Jesus of Nazareth" on my forehead with my thumb, all the terror, horror, and trembling vanished. The next night he shook my flesh with burning, horror, and pain so that I could barely stand. But just as before, I felt no fear after the first movement, and all of a sudden every phantom of the enemy vanished.

If anyone should think this was the spirit of some dead person who had come to ask for help, but could not speak unless I had first spoken to him[108]—I don't think so. For I don't believe such a spirit would have departed without success on both nights, given that I was so eager to assist a human spirit from purgatory. That's why I said this seemed to be a devil.

32. On thoughts sent by the devil

Seeing that he had gained nothing, the devil sent me good thoughts, for he wanted me to write them as revelations in a little book I composed, *On the Name of Mary and the Sacrament of the Altar.*[109] Even though they had been sent by the devil, I believed they were good all the same, so I would have written them down—but I was compelled to write otherwise, yielding voluntarily to the Holy Spirit. When I wondered about this, I was shown by revelation that the glorious Virgin would not let me write anything in her book that had come from the devil—even if it seemed good in itself.

Later on, I realized in a true illumination that, when we interpret this name *Mary*, we can understand that sinners are illumined in three ways, depending on how we interpret "illumined." Some grieve bitterly[110] because they feel no perceptible grief for their sins. Others do grieve with perceptible grief. Still others grieve because they are delayed from the kingdom of God. Yet they too are sinners, for we all offend in many ways.[111]

---

108. A common belief about ghosts, that is, spirits from purgatory who come to ask the living for suffrages.

109. This treatise does not survive.

110. *amare dolent.* The name *Maria* is sometimes derived from *amara* (bitter). Cf. Ruth 1:20.

111. Jas 3:2.

Sometimes at the mere thought of laying down my body, my heart melts from the touch of the Spirit of wisdom. Then my heart seems to hear rumors, in that spiritual sensation, that some great new thing is about to happen—and I expect to die very soon. May God happily grant this! And I want it to happen in a special, miraculous way to set an example of holiness for the whole world. I desire this not to be especially praised (my witness is God, from whom no secret is hid), but to stir all people to the most perfect love of God—not just those who know me and live near me, but all mortals throughout the world. For that reason, too, in order to be of profit to all through the melting of my soul, I desire to hold office over all.[112] Otherwise I detest that idea! Again, he from whom nothing is hidden is my witness; I often tell him these things in the spirit. Praise to him forever and ever!

33. On true desire, or yearning to be dissolved and be with Christ[113]

On the feast of Saint Nicholas the bishop,[114] I celebrated a Mass of the Blessed Virgin at the high altar, this being my duty to the order. When I had come to the prayers of preparation before receiving the Eucharist, I began as usual to ask God to deliver me from this world with his holy call, for I languish for love.[115] This is my daily preparation, although I have seven special preparatory meditations according to Scripture, and I read all of them as appropriate. They unfold over the course of a week, and the cycle begins on Sunday. These preparatory meditations have the text, "Come to me, all you who desire me, and take your fill of my

---

112. *Cupio prelatiam omnium portare.* Methley perhaps alludes to the Benedictine Rule, chap. 64, which says the abbot's role is more to profit his monks than to preside over them (*prodesse magis quam praeesse*).

113. Phil 1:23.

114. December 6.

115. Song 2:5.

fruits,"[116] and so forth. So as I was thinking about the words "Come to me," all of a sudden a perceptible love and languor came upon me. Illumined and urged on in the spirit, I spoke these words to the One who had come to me, for I somehow welcomed the Beloved as he came to that place. But I say "somehow," like one who stands beside the Beloved when he is sought and invoked, yet he seems not to answer. And yet he says, "Before you call upon me, I will say 'Here I am.' "[117] So I said to him, "I truly long for you and desire to cross over to you from this world. But I cannot, for I am confined in this putrid body that I bear as if in prison." And my heart melted like wax before the fire.[118]

34. On having firm hope in the blessed Virgin

On the vigil of the Conception of the blessed Virgin Mother of God,[119] I began a little work called *Three Ways of Excellence*, containing three books.[120] The first book, already complete, is about the Virgin's compassion, the second about the excellence of her grief and her love. I chose that theme because some people write that, perfect as she was, she had no grief that others could discern and shed no tears. And I proved that [if this were true], it should be ascribed to imperfection rather than perfection.[121] For Christ himself shed tears in his passion, and his sweat became like drops of blood falling on the ground.[122]

116. Sir 24:26.
117. Isa 58:9.
118. Ps 67:3.
119. The feast of the Immaculate Conception (which was not universally observed) falls on December 8.
120. *Triuium Excellencie*, another lost work.
121. A debate within late medieval Mariology, visible in sacred art as well. Some depicted the Virgin as so perfectly conformed to the will of God that she displayed no outward grief, while others represented her as both demonstrating and deserving profound compassion, as in the famous sequence *Stabat mater*. It is not surprising that the intensely emotional Methley belongs to the second group.
122. Luke 22:44.

After None, that is, at midday, when I had said the Office of the Dead (*Placebo, Dirige,* and so forth) as required, I came to the passage where it is written, "In this I knew that you desired me, for my enemy will not rejoice over me."[123] Suddenly I gazed at the stone image of the Virgin on the altar in my cell and felt a touch of divine love. Following my spiritual instinct, I said to her, "In this I knew," and so forth. "So I place my hope in you with firm trust that you will help me in the best way possible to bring this book to a good end." And so, thanks to her, it was finished.

35. Another example of hope in the glorious Virgin

I composed another short work of which I spoke earlier: *On the Name of Mary and Reception of the Eucharist.*[124] Because I suffered from a physical problem that interfered with my spiritual peace, I told her that if she helped me and took it away, I would compose that little work for her. When I had come around to writing the work, she gradually relieved my ailment, I don't know how. By the time I had completely finished the work, I sensed that I was cured. Thanks be to God and Mary forever and ever!

36. On a thought about the transgression of our first father Adam

On the Sunday after the feast of the glorious Virgin's blessed conception, I had read at table in the refectory while my brothers sat and ate. In the sermon I was reading, this text happened to occur: "A heavy yoke upon all the children of Adam."[125] Suddenly my heart was moved as if struck by a sword.[126] Melting with love and pain, I contemplated what a heavy yoke I bear from the first father Adam onwards—and not only I, but everyone. Even those

123. Ps 40:12.
124. The same lost work mentioned in chap. 32 above, with a variant title.
125. Sir 40:1.
126. Cf. Luke 2:35.

who pay no attention, or take little account of it, are all the more heavily oppressed the less attention they pay. As I felt myself stirred this way in the spirit, I did not want to willfully abandon the reading and the brothers on account of that sensation, unless the spirit and the fervor of love and pain were to work even more strongly in me. If fervor is so great that it causes ecstasy, it over-rules command of the body and suddenly deprives the lover of self-control, so he must yield to the spirit. But if it is slow and can be governed, he should not be so aroused (except by a special impulse) that he cannot complete the work he is supposed to do.

37. On the free call of contemplation, on laying down the body, and on contingent needs or the inaccurate writing of books

On the day after the feast of Saint Eulalia, the virgin martyr,[127] when I was in my cell at Compline and just about to say the Creed ("I believe in God the Father"), the devil tempted me. He told me I should not wish to be dissolved and be with Christ because I had books that I had corrected before, yet I came back to them later and found that something was still inaccurate—a word, a syllable, a letter, perhaps a title or something of that sort. So he said I should delay and correct them again. And look! While I was saying the Creed, I was suddenly illumined in spirit and saw that I should not for that reason give up my chaste desire to lay down my body, to obtain Christ purely for his own sake. Since those who are led by the Spirit of God are children of God,[128] I saw that if God were to take a mortal man from the body to himself through the force of exceptional grief and love, [he would attend] not only to his soul, but also to the correction of books and every other need, whatever it might be.[129] For it is impossible that divine aid should fail God's elect when human aid fails.

---

127. This feast falls on December 10.

128. Rom 8:14.

129. This fascinating anecdote shows that Methley corrected his own books, though imperfectly, and helps to explain the poor state of the manuscript.

During the celebration of Mass I very often desire to be dissolved and be with Christ, and the enemy objects on account of present need. But I reply: he will either complete the sacrifice or assist the priest whom the Lord provides for that purpose. And the same rule applies in all other similar cases. Yet we must beware at other times (and even at this time) not to spoil anything by our own will. For man was created to serve God in body and spirit, with all his powers and senses, movements, thoughts, and words.

38. On diabolical temptation and divine consolation

On the day before the feast of Saint Lucy, the glorious virgin martyr,[130] I rose for Matins, not at midnight but two hours earlier, as the Carthusian custom is nowadays.[131] Troubled by the chilly weather, my sensuality[132] was grumbling, and the enemy, vicious as he is, saw this and added pain to pain. I thought how I could provide a remedy or protect myself from him, for he had caused my pain with his deception and falseness when he kept me from wearing a cloak to defend myself against the cold. Knowing that I was threatened by the enemy's violence, I raised myself up against him and fought bravely all night long with all my strength, to the best of my meager ability. As the fight was vigorous and intense on both sides, he saw that he had gained no advantage. After changing his mode of temptation again and again, he finally returned to his original method. At last, weighed down with sleep after Matins, I had some rest from his attack. When I rose for Prime, I cast out every alien thought that did not tend directly toward God; that is, I rejected wandering thoughts about any other thing. Soon I was caught up in spiritual melody. Rejoicing in Jesus throughout the dawn hour, I was consoled with as much peace in

130. The feast is December 13.

131. As of the general chapter of 1423.

132. *Sensualitas mea*, referring to the physical constitution of the body. Cf. Julian of Norwich's Middle English term *sensualite*.

God as I had been assaulted before by the devil's temptation. Thanks to the Beloved forever and ever!

39. On awaiting the will of God and preparing the mind to obey him at all times, giving itself to whatever task he wills

As I was at Mass the same day, holding the sacrament in order to receive it, I began as usual to speak words of love to Christ. Suddenly—by the enemy's guile, if I'm not mistaken—it occurred to me that I might speak to him with mocking irony, not in words but in spirit. "You truly desire to be with him in love! In fact, you are afraid that he might speak to you in the spirit. Then you would have some revelation that you would have to write down, distracting you from your other work."[133] Casting this temptation far from me, I felt myself truly free in spirit for whatever task I wanted to take up. Just as before it was necessary to be on guard against vices and to labor in good works, so afterward one must cease from good works and serve the will of God in whatever task he chooses.[134]

40. On the hidden judgment of God and how it helps the lover

After None on the same day (the day before the feast of Saint Lucy), I was devoutly meditating on the fact that no one knows how he will pass from this world—how or when he will die, in what condition, or with what merits. I also knew of one reason for this, namely, a person should be prepared at all times and hope in God. Suddenly I began to think about the hidden judgment of God. Without God a person can do nothing; it is by his grace that

---

133. Cf. chap. 11 above. Methley perceived some tension between the act of contemplation itself and the need to write about it.

134. An idea found in many mystics. Beginners must struggle constantly to resist vices and do good works, but more advanced contemplatives should abandon their own agenda (however virtuous) and open themselves to the will of God as it unfolds in every moment.

anyone turns away from evil and does good. And no one can penetrate God's hidden judgment—why he draws one person by his grace but does not draw another, who has not received grace. Yet if a person has received grace and done good, it must be ascribed to God, its author. At once I received an answer through enlightened reason. Even if a person cannot penetrate this mystery, he can still know that it gives him an occasion to love God, seeing that he can do nothing good without him. Thus he sees that he must tenderly love the one from whom he has received grace so that he can fear him, serve him, and enjoy him (even here) in eternal peace.

41. How we should admire and embrace the mercy of God toward all humankind

On the Saturday before the third Sunday of Advent in the same year, 1487, I was sitting in choir at Matins in the middle of the night. This passage from the prophet Isaiah was being read: "It is I who blot out your iniquities for my own sake, and I will not remember your sins."[135] Suddenly, as this word of God through the prophet rang in my ears, my heart was softened and melted by the sweetness of love, as I considered how we should embrace his wonderful mercy toward humankind. It is clear from these words how mercifully he receives a person who truly repents, without feigning—not only in words and speech, but in deed and in truth.[136] For he speaks not only once but twice, giving the great confidence of love. This doubling of the word confirms [repentance with both] the voice and the truthful heart, without feigning. When he says "for my own sake," it means that he blots out a sinner's iniquities by the grace of his own goodness, for the sinner in himself does not deserve grace. Therefore God gives him prevenient grace for the sake of his own goodness, saying, "Even if

---

135. Isa 43:25.
136. 1 Tim 1:5; 1 John 3:18.

it is not for your sake, yet for my own sake I blot out your iniquities, because I am good." Well then—after this, why will I not remember your sins? This is what is written in another prophet: "On that day you will not be put to shame for all your wicked deeds by which you have connived against me."[137] He gives abundantly to all and does not reproach. Instead, he blots out sins so that in the future, they cannot rise up to fill the heart with shame. "I will sing the Lord's mercies forever" in love,[138] remembering how mercifully he dealt with me on earth when he said, "It is I who blot out your iniquities for my own sake, and I will not remember your sins."

See, dearest brothers, I have written this *Refectory of Salvation* for you. Correct it if necessary, give thanks to God, and pray for me. If you have written well, correct what you have written; otherwise, I ask you not to write.[139] Praise and honor to God!

Here ends *The Refectory of Salvation*, composed from the most opulent drunkenness by that man of God, Richard Methley, filled with delights.

137. Zeph 3:11.
138. Ps 88:2.
139. Methley here uses the same verb, *scribere*, for both composing and copying. But he asks scribes who are unwilling to correct his text not to copy it at all. Cf. chap. 37 above.

The Experience of Truth

Only the second half of this text is extant.
The manuscript begins near the opening of chapter 14.

14. [On guardian angels]

. . . each of us has an angel personally assigned to us. We can prove this from a passage in Scripture: the Lord sent his angel and released Peter from prison, and when they had walked down one street, the angel left him. Peter came to the others who were gathered in the house of Mark the evangelist's mother. But when he knocked at the door, the hearers did not at first believe him, for they said, "It is his angel." As it seems to me, this refers to his personal angel,[1] assigned to him by God until death. For they did not believe that he was present then and there in the body. In addition, the apostle Paul says, "To keep me from being too elated by the magnitude of revelations, a goad was given me in my flesh—an angel of Satan to harass me. Three times I prayed to God about this, asking that it should depart from me," and so forth.[2] We can take this to mean that God has given everyone not only a good angel, but also a bad one: the good one to provide help, the other to exercise him with temptation.[3] But in the meantime, whenever God wills and it is fitting, he sends others, good or bad, who are not personally assigned until death like the others. Rather, they remain with us as long as God wills or (in the case of bad ones) permits.

1. Acts 12:6-15.
2. 2 Cor 12:7-8.
3. A widespread belief. Cf. Caesarius of Heisterbach, *Dialogus miraculorum* V.1 and VII.44.

Whether it is an angel assigned to us personally or others who attend for a time, none of them are deprived of the vision of God because of their ministry. All of them (as the apostle Paul the hierarch[4] says) can be called "ministering spirits sent forth to serve, for the sake of those who are to inherit salvation."[5] For God is whole in every place, so he whose vision is the glory of the saints can be seen by them everywhere. As for bad angels, wherever they may be, they doubtless carry their punishment with them in a way, for their malice torments them. They are never entirely without pain; indeed, they are kept in great pain. I should say rather that they are tortured by envy.

God is truly closer to his lover than any creature is, for he not only holds sway in his heart or conscience, but chiefly abides in his soul itself, if it is pure. Even after the death of a sinner, the divine image somehow remains in the soul. Woe to the person who departs from the God that loves him so! But let us return to our purpose.

15. How many ways a good or bad angel speaks to a person, or a person speaks to himself

I will explain as best I can, with God's guidance, what I have learned from experience about these good and bad angels—how they can speak and in how many ways. First I will explain the ways a good angel speaks or appears. Whether it is the angel assigned to a person or one sent just for a time, a good angel utters words like a human being. But if anyone asks how it looks, I say that it cannot always be seen in person, although its voice is heard. Sometimes, too, it appears spiritually, yet one cannot always tell if the speaker is an angel or God himself except by asking. Even if a person asks, the voice sometimes answers that its identity must not be known. An angel once replied to my question this

---

4. *Ab apostolo gerarcha paolo*, an unusual epithet for the Apostle.
5. Heb 1:14.

way: "As the church holds concerning Moses and John the Evangelist, so you should believe concerning this voice." Sometimes the angel sends thoughts[6] and sometimes it appears physically, showing itself to a person's bodily eyes as if it too were embodied. But I myself have never experienced this.

A bad angel too appears or speaks in the same ways: sometimes invisibly, sometimes visibly, and in the other ways I have mentioned. At times I have seen them myself with my bodily eyes in a great many ways. A bad angel can assume the forms of human beings in just about every station or walk of life—men and women, wild beasts, sheep and cattle, poor men and rich—in order to delude and deceive. But none has ever prevailed against me by such means, thanks be to God.

A person can also speak to himself in his own mind, somehow articulating an idea in his conscience or his reason. I will add this: sometimes a person has a premonition in his heart (he does not know whence it comes) that something will or will not happen, as if he knew this by a spirit of prophecy. So he says, [God] gives me knowledge in my heart, or in my mind, that this or that will happen. Similarly in prayer, when people anxiously weep about a petition and later find themselves calm, they feel a sensation in their heart that God has granted their prayer. But they do not know how or when, unless by chance they devoutly believe that also. To hope in such things is not beyond the bounds of our salvation.

Now, if I'm not mistaken, I have briefly explained how many ways a locution can come to a person from a good or bad angel, or even from himself. I will also say how, insofar as I can.

16. On thoughts sent by good and bad angels, and on union, cognition, and sensation

As I have said, the words of good and bad angels have the same sound and meaning as human words. But as for the thoughts they

---

6. *Aliquando per immissisonem* (for *immissionem*).

send, we must take diligent note of how they come about. A good angel sends good thoughts, for it moves or encourages the mind to remember or ask the beloved God for something useful, just as if one person were urging another to do something. It does not compel, however, but encourages through words or signs. Similarly, a bad angel prompts bad thoughts. Sometimes they are mingled with good ones—but it always sends them for a bad end, at an inappropriate time. This frequently happens during the Divine Office. We must also say this about thoughts sent by angels.[7] Some people think the angel speaks with them according to its essence, but in fact, this cannot be true. An angel does not speak with a person in every possible way, but only in certain ways: through union,[8] through application, or (if it is a bad angel) through oppression. For God alone can fill a creature according to his essence. Some people are said to have pythonic spirits in their bellies or their breast,[9] but even if that is true physically, it cannot be true essentially in the soul.

If a good angel teaches through a revelation or vision, its teaching is often accompanied by ecstasy or rapture. In other words, the person who speaks with the angel experiences either full rapture or ecstasy, which is a certain alienation of the mind. I do not call it madness, but the mind is alienated [from the senses], so it cannot pay attention to anything that would interfere with its hearing or understanding. But sometimes such a person experiences hardly any rapture or ecstasy, especially if his senses are habitually trained in the discernment of good and evil.[10] Similarly, a bad angel causes its own kind of ecstasy or rapture, but it is not the

7. *Immissiones itaque cognoscentes dicendum occurrit.* The text is corrupt.

8. *Per vnicionem* rather than *vnionem.* Methley does not define these terms. *Oppressio* is harassment by a demon.

9. A biblical way of referring to divination through evil spirits: Lev 20:27; Deut 18:11; 1 Sam 28:7; Acts 16:16. On demons in the bowels, see Nancy Caciola, *Discerning Spirits: Divine and Demonic Possession in the Middle Ages* (Ithaca, NY: Cornell University Press, 2003), 197, 200, 213.

10. Heb 5:14.

same. The two can be distinguished in this way: a good angel reveals its teaching clearly, a bad angel obscurely. It is not completely obscure, but only in comparison with the good angel.

If inexperienced persons cannot distinguish them by this means, there is another, better way to tell if the angels are evil. A good angel always provides material for rejoicing about good things or devoutly weeping about punishments [for sin]. Whether or not the angel speaks, this sensation brings such a sweet savor to the mind, as I said above, that it changes a person's spiritual state and makes the will entirely good. This rule never fails. In fact, there is a kind of familiar speech among angels that does not always cause such great sweetness, but it always produces some kind of devotion.

A bad angel either openly urges a person to carnal pleasures or makes him think bad thoughts about spiritual things, that is, the pleasures of the mind, under color of something good. I say simply that they can be known by their raptures and the sweetness of their taste. For a bad angel too offers its phony sweetness or melodies to the senses of smell, taste, and hearing, and it often tries to give fervor to preachers. But it is not finally permitted to deceive the simple, the humble, and the prudent, because a good person never consents to such things without seeking the judgment of someone wiser. Whether such locutions are spoken truly or falsely, they benefit and profit a wise person. If they move his affections to any degree, he entrusts this to God, for he does not fully discern or judge how such things come about—unless he clearly knows without error.

17. What questions should be asked about persons who have visions or hear [locutions]

Now if anyone asks what should be done when someone receives a striking revelation, so that hearers want to know if it is true or false, I say there are five things to discern so as to know the truth openly. First, the character of the person; next, that of the vision; third, that of the revealer; fourth, the manner; and fifth, the character of the transformation, translation, or rapture [experienced by the seer].[11]

The character of persons must be discerned. We need to know if they are devout or sinful, if they are credible, or if there is good reason for doubt. Can we believe these people are not afraid to lie, or would they rather be killed than knowingly proclaim a falsehood? Before I proceed any further, let me say that if such a person is constant and truthful, and has the perceptible divine love that I discussed above, I simply affirm that he or she should be believed.[12] For no one can by any means err in this divine love.

Second, the character of the vision must be discerned. I dare not claim that God gives the sweetness of devotion to great sinners and shows them heavenly visions. Rather, he gives them visions of judgment or the pains of purgatory or hell. But if the person is devout, I affirm that visions of both kinds can occur and are frequently shown.

Third, the quality of the revealer should be considered. Does the vision or locution come from God or an angel? If an angel, is it a good or a bad one? If it comes from God or a good angel, I simply affirm that it should be believed. Yet I admit some room for doubt, for the mode or time when the vision will be fulfilled is often unknown, unless this is expressly stated. If the vision or locution comes from a bad angel, its truth or falsehood must be discerned. If it is false, the person who sees or hears it should be warned. If it is true (which often happens), the visionary should be warned all the more against future errors. For an evil spirit says or reveals true things in order to gain credence so that later, when he reveals falsehoods, he will not be recognized, apprehended, or

11. The first three questions are proposed by Jean Gerson in his well-known treatise on discernment, *De probatione spirituum*. Gerson is considerably more skeptical than Methley.

12. Although the first half of this treatise is lost, Methley discusses "perceptible divine love" (*sensibilem diuinum amorem*) at length in his other works.

seen [as evil]. Let me also state here something I left out above.[13] The enemy's face always reveals his cunning, especially the eyes, in my experience. For his eyes are despicable even if he appears radiant with precious gems and golden robes, like a king or queen.

Fourth, the mode of the vision must be discerned. Did it take place in ecstasy or in rapture? Was it a spiritual, an intellectual, or a corporeal vision?[14] If these types of vision are properly interpreted in their place, I believe the books of contemplatives always say that ecstasy and spiritual vision assume the forms of objects in the spirit. If it is a pure rapture (that is, an intellectual vision), there are no visible forms. What is visible to the eyes is a corporeal vision.

The fifth thing to discern is the quality of transformation, translation, or rapture (all these terms mean the same thing in this context). That is, we should ask whether the visionary experienced full rapture with sweetness, or only a certain alteration of the mind, or dry devotion.[15] If it was full rapture with sweetness, I affirm that the vision is true. If not, I have doubts. Now I have briefly explained what questions should be asked, but I have still more to say.

18. On the evangelists and prophets of modern times,[16] and the deceits of the devil

Everyone who speaks as an evangelist or a prophet does so on the grounds of a revelation he has seen or heard. If he speaks as an

13. *Marginal note*: see chap. 6.

14. The three classic types of vision, identified by Augustine in *De Genesi ad litteram*, cap. 12. Augustine says that only intellectual or imageless visions can never deceive. "Spiritual visions" are also called "imaginative visions" because they involve mental images.

15. *desecata deuocione*, perhaps for *desiccata*.

16. Hogg and Clarke point out that there were prophets at Mount Grace itself. John Norton, Methley's religious brother, said Christ had promised him that there would be thirty-three charterhouses in England. Norton's scribe, Dom Robert Fletcher, was reported as late as 1534 to be having revelations. *The Works*, p. 115.

evangelist—that is, if he gives a plain account—we should see if it accords with the catholic faith. For example, if someone were to say that some condition within the church is sinful, perhaps because they have changed the traditions of the ancient fathers, the opinions of theologians must be consulted to reach a decision in accord with God and conscience. We should always choose what is better, safer, and kinder. For absolutely no mortal is allowed to compose statutes, even at a general council, by which the souls of those who follow them could be damned or harmed.[17]

If such a person speaks as a prophet, we must see if what he says about past, present but hidden, and also future things should be accepted.[18] If he speaks [truthfully] about events in the past that are completely unknown to him, he should be believed as long as he does not contradict the faith. In this way we can discover that he has prophesied, even if he says he only heard a voice but saw no vision and learned nothing by other means, except through the teaching of God or an angel. I am assuming it was a good angel, not a bad one, and I understand in the same way if he prophesies about present and future things.

But if a bad angel wants to make a person foretell the future or prophesy, he should neither be entirely believed nor entirely contradicted. His case stands somewhere in the middle, if nothing can be clearly discerned beyond a doubt. If [the prophet] wants to follow my advice, he will trick the devil and make him fight against himself. Here is an analogy. If the mother of a toddler realizes that her child is outside in the street, or perhaps in the

17. Methley speaks with regard to the conciliar movement. On competing political revelations see Renate Blumenfeld-Kosinski, *Poets, Saints, and Visionaries of the Great Schism, 1378–1417* (Philadelphia: University of Pennsylvania Press, 2006).

18. According to Gregory the Great, a prophet may reveal hidden truths about the past and the present (for example, the secrets of another's heart), as well as the future. *Homiliae in Hiezechihelem Prophetam* I.1–3, ed. Marcus Adriaen, CCSL 142 (Turnhout: Brepols, 1971), 5–7.

garden where there is a well or some other danger, she gets up to look for him and keep him safe. She does not act out of wicked suspicion but from true compassion, shaken to her core (so to speak) because she had forgotten her child. If he is safe, well and good. But if she finds him dead, she says that something utterly terrible has happened to her.

So too with the man of God. Suppose a wicked angel tells him someone is in a state of sin, and that spirit rejoices because the sinner has not come to his senses. The man of God does not know if this is true. Yet, prompted by true pity to correct his brother, he can rise and go to him in any way the Holy Spirit teaches him at the time, and ask if he happens to be in the danger that the devil announced. If he is, he can be helped. If not, let him be glad of it, and they can both give thanks to God. But if the case is found to be just as the devil said and the remedy of correction can be applied, then the enemy has lost both of them—for he had thought he could possess the one through his sin and the other through his prideful judgment. We must act this way in order to be forewarned and forearmed in everything. That is how the devil's illusion can be unmasked: do not believe him until the truth can be proven. If evil is found, let it be corrected so no one will be at risk.

19. How a false evangelist can be caught if two or more contradict each other

Someone might ask what should be done if two people have contradictory revelations about the same thing, whether they are prophets (predicting things that are hidden) or evangelists (preaching things that are public). I will say what I think should be done in such a case. This can be understood by analogy, at least in part, for we read in the Old Testament that it happened with respect to prophecy, and we know the ends of both sides. Jeremiah, Micah, and other prophets were clearly proven true in the end, and their adversaries were put to shame. But since no one knows what is the case with a person except God and that person's own spirit,[19] how can the truth be proven (and the problem solved) until the outcome is known? I think it is impossible, or at least very difficult. Yet I will say this: truth has no part in falsehood. If one person simply denies what the other affirms in all respects, or without exception, one of them is certainly false. But I will explain as best I can what to do in this dilemma—first with respect to evangelists.[20]

If one person says that such-and-such a matter (which he names) has not been rightly defined, and another on the contrary says it is indeed right, "and this has been revealed to me in the spirit," one of them is surely in error. If possible, let each person's way of life be investigated secretly. One who simply glories in God, and therefore affirms nothing beyond what he truly knows, cannot be deceived as long as he remains in that state. But the one who is deceived surely does not glory in God, but seeks pleasure elsewhere in some creature. If this is not obvious in public, perhaps he can be caught in secret. If so, he is undoubtedly deceived, for the Holy Spirit by no means coexists with pretense.[21] If by chance the one who is caught out wants to be reconciled but thinks his conscience will not allow it, he should know for certain that this is from the devil. Therefore the Apostle rightly says, "if in prophecy, in accord with the rule of faith,"[22] and again, "Let the spirits of prophets be subject to prophets."[23] This rule should be followed not only in prophecy, but in everything, even if a person believes he is the most truthful evangelist. So in a way, you can compel the spirit who speaks evil by urging him to be silent and subject. He can by no means compel you against your will. This

---

19. Cf. 1 Cor 2:11.

20. The "false evangelists" in Methley's view were probably Lollards, though if this treatise is late, they could have been Lutherans.

21. *cum ficcione*.

22. Rom 12:6.

23. 1 Cor 14:32.

is a good kind of stubbornness: not to consent to the devil in any way, but to say mentally just once, "You will keep the peace"— and hold him to it.

20. Who should be believed, even without a sign, if prophets contradict each other

If two prophets contradict each other, it is hard to discern the truth before the future event that one predicted and the other denied— and perhaps even after it. But here is what sometimes happens, I think—or there is surely no doubt that it *could* happen. If one prophet announces a future sign and another denies it, or says it was revealed by the devil, and the sign then occurs—ask whether it might have occurred by God's permission or his providence, as in the case of rain, snow, winds, and the like. The devil is some- times shrewd about such things. Or if the secrets of a person's conscience are revealed to someone, that too could be shown by the devil (unless it is against the person's will),[24] for the devil knows the consciences of many. So is there any sign whose truth no one should doubt if it comes to pass? Indeed, I know of none. Yet if such a sign occurs and cannot be doubted, I do not deny that the prophet should be believed. This is the case especially if he predicted the precise time of the future event.

If a prophet predicts no sign, but simply affirms that something was revealed to him in the spirit, I think he should be believed sooner than the one who predicts a sign, for we cannot know for certain if the sign was a lucky guess or was truly revealed by God. In all these things, if the person who prophesies or evangelizes says that he experienced a true, perceptible transformation of his mind in divine love, and his conscience is such that he would never knowingly lie, then the ones to whom he has been sent should believe him—whether or not he predicts a sign. For just

24. *nisi sit contra hominem.*

as God or a good angel cannot possibly lie, no one in such a state of grace can evangelize or prophesy other than truthfully.

21. What a holy man should do if he is asked to settle a dispute among theologians

If theologians who are debating some matter should ask a holy man for the truth—not because they have doubts about the faith, but because they cannot reach a consensus—here is what I think the man of God should do in this difficulty.[25] I will speak briefly, God willing, as best I can. First, let him know that even if the theologians do not understand the question, the elect in Christ's church know things that lesser souls may not be allowed to know,[26] even if the question must finally be referred to the Roman Curia. But perhaps the theologians want to hear or read what the holy man himself thinks. So if he wants to be secure, let him proceed in this way.

In spiritual things, God often reveals his will to his elect in accord with wisdom, that is, savory knowledge,[27] which consists in perceptible love. But he does not always show them how to express what they have learned in the spirit in literal terms. The man of God should also know that sometimes, what is appropriate as a general rule does not help someone who follows it as an individual. Knowing these things, let the holy man seek a solution through prayer, not reading. Perhaps when he least expects it—because by that time, he may even have forgotten the matter—God will reveal it to him by one of the aforesaid ways. But let him beware of simply

25. These theologians (*doctores*) are scholastics. It would be interesting to know how often Methley and his fellow Carthusians received such requests. In the thirteenth and fourteenth centuries, such dilemmas were often set before holy women, but by Methley's day only men would be trusted to attain privileged insight.

26. *tamen ecclesia christi scit in electis si non liceat nesciri ad minus.*

27. *sapienciam, id est sapidam scienciam.* The noun *sapientia* (wisdom) is linked etymologically with the verb *sapio, sapere,* to taste.

proposing his own explanation, unless he indicates this by saying, "It seems to me that such-and-such should be accepted." Rather, let him simply tell what he has seen, heard, or known in the illumination of his intellect, because learned men should examine not only the vision, but also the mode of understanding.[28]

With the aforesaid signs, or at least one of them—perceptible love given by God—the holy man cannot err. But without it, he can know nothing with certainty except by chance. For just as God and his servants are of one mind, whether they are celestial like the angels or earthly and embodied, like hermits and holy men, they share one way of life in perceptible love. Without this, as I have said, it is impossible to know the truth; with it, it is impossible to err. God never teaches error, and the devil never gives divine love. A person can know by his sensation whose love he experiences.[29]

22. What the man of God should do when he sees that he is contradicted or not believed by others

But what should he do in the meantime if he sees that others do not believe him? He knows that he knows the truth, for love has taught him. Along with the truth, love gives everything that is needed to defend it—knowledge, constancy, compassion, and so forth. I will explain as best I can, and in order to speak well, I will first offer a Hail Mary.

Divine revelation is the firmament of the human heart and the full proof of faith. It was by divine illumination and revelation that Moses, the prophets,[30] and David the psalmist learned what they handed down to us in Scripture as worthy of belief. Therefore

---

28. Methley shows deep respect for the *doctores*. The holy man must not try to pawn off his own theological opinion as divine revelation, and if he does, he deserves to be challenged.

29. *Sensacio* refers to a subtle, inward spiritual perception.

30. Cf. Luke 16:29.

the catholic faith is clearly known from sacred Scripture, which was revealed to these men by the inspiration of God. Moreover, the apostles Peter and Paul handed down to us in their epistles that they had firm faith in the Scriptures and in divine revelation. This is clear in 2 Peter,[31] 2 Corinthians,[32] and Galatians, where Paul said that even if an angel from heaven were to preach a gospel contrary to the one he taught, it would be accursed.[33] And surely his heart was confirmed in the firmness of faith by divine revelation, vision, and inspiration. The Son of God himself, who is the only foundation that anyone can lay,[34] affirmed that holy Scripture was given by God to establish firm faith: "If he called them 'gods' to whom the word of God was given, and Scripture cannot be broken, then what of him whom the Father consecrated and sent into the world?"[35]

So it should be with you, man of God. If you find that your vision concurs with sacred Scripture and you know that you experienced perceptible love, then all flesh cannot shake you as long as you live and breathe, even if others do not believe you. But in everything you do, believe with the faith of your soul. If they allege against you that others have been deceived before, know this: it does not follow that you too are deceived. Many people today are aware that some have been deceived in the past, so they do not believe God's modern prophets. This is especially the case if they prophesy against their own errors, for such people take little care to recognize and correct them. Yet some have learned from experience that the things I write about are true, so they have been compelled to believe.

As for you, speak when God bids you speak and be silent when he does not. For the sake of your soul, do not be ashamed to speak the truth in a time of need. In everything of this kind, the Holy Spirit

31. 2 Pet 1:20-21.
32. 2 Cor 11:4.
33. Gal 1:8.
34. 1 Cor 3:11.
35. John 10:35-36.

will teach you if there is no human being you can trust in spiritual matters. Yet beware of rash judgment and discern well, in keeping with the time and manner [of your revelation]. A person's mind or spiritual state can change for better or worse in the twinkling of an eye. So as the Holy Spirit teaches you, be silent, or else entrust the revelation to your superiors for their judgment. There is no doubt that the One who created you can teach you rightly. But in all these things, if you receive a divine revelation by any good means, attend diligently to what I have said—for evil never comes from God.

23. On bishops and pastors who want to move to a hermitage

Some people may be prompted by the Spirit to go to a place of quiet, having legitimately laid aside their pastoral responsibilities. Others may wish to leave the quiet [of the hermitage] to take on a pastoral role, not knowing whether this impulse comes from a good or a bad spirit—always putting the catholic faith first.[36] I will reply to these men briefly in the present work because I have given a fuller response elsewhere, especially in *A Defense of the Solitary or Contemplative Life*, which is meant for pastors who wish to depart.[37]

I say that where the Spirit of the Lord is, there is freedom.[38] It is therefore God who is calling, and such a man should undoubtedly go to the hermitage if he can do so canonically. If anyone asks when God is calling, see what I have said above. In several passages I have explained how God or an angel may speak in many ways. But if God inspires the will to go to a hermitage, yet does not want that desire to be fulfilled, he often gives the will without the ability. If you ask how this can be recognized, I will explain as best I can.

36. According to canon law, one could transfer from a more relaxed form of religious life to a stricter one, but not vice versa. Hence Methley argues that a pastor or even a bishop can become a Carthusian (the strictest life), but the reverse is not possible.

37. A lost work by Methley.

38. 2 Cor 3:17.

If there are canonical reasons that impede such a pastor, it will appear that the move is not fitting. Then the desire will be accepted in place of the deed because the actual deed is not possible. If you want me to tell you what those reasons are, or at least one of them, they are hard to define. But I will say what I think can be discovered. The Lord Jesus Christ, the chief of pastors, preached to the Jews—and they crucified him, on the authority of Pontius Pilate and the soldiers who served under him. Yet the Pharisees, whose way of life was evil, edified the people by preaching the law of God. I have used these examples to show that good teachers cannot always profit the people, yet bad ones sometimes do. Suppose that a good bishop finds that his preaching is unprofitable, for the most part. Yet when he is wrongfully removed, many may come to their senses, inspired by God. If God should call that bishop by inspiration or in some other way, let him go to the hermitage with the consent, or at least the knowledge and permission, of the lord pope.

Both a good and a bad pastor can profit the people—sometimes a bad one, sometimes a good. If experience clearly shows that the people will perish if their pastor departs, this reason impedes him, even if he has a good and inspired will [to become a hermit]. So whether the preacher is a good pastor or a bad one, he profits the people if God inspires him. Another good man may legitimately depart if God and the lord pope are willing.

24. *What spirit prompts a man who wants to move from a quiet life to preaching*

Consider another man who lives in solitude, which is by no means solicitude. If on his own initiative he wants to leave or actually does leave, he will err. Whether he was led by a good spirit or a bad one (not that I should say this),[39] he entered the hermitage or the strict religious life, so he ought to keep his vow and in that way change his bad intention into a good one. I do not deny that

---

39. Reading *ne dicam* for *ve dicam*.

God might inspire him [to depart], but I do not believe he would ever bring that desire to fruition. In that case it is undoubtedly enough for the hermit zealously to will [a life of preaching]. For the rest, even if he has such a desire, it is better for him to persevere in the solitary or religious life as long as he lives. But if God leads him to the governance of souls with no initiative on his own part, it will appear that a good angel has indeed visited him, not a bad one, or that God has inspired him.

What if someone contradicts this and says a man can have himself excused from the hermitage or the religious life in order to preach, acting on his own initiative? Unless there is greater need than I have ever heard of or read in any book, I say he is deceived by the devil—or else he has never experienced the love of God. For beyond a doubt, no one who has experienced it would ever consent to leave, even if God revealed to him that he wanted him to preach. He would have to be dragged away by the forceful insistence of others, not by his own efforts. Alas, for pity! In that case he would have a great and wondrous inner struggle, desiring with his whole heart to fulfill the divine command and not merely to be overcome by human reason. To receive the care of souls or to preach—because of the honor or the labor it involves, because of the anxiety it causes, because he would be delayed from seeing the Beloved in his kingdom (the One he yearns to contemplate, not just in a mystery or a celestial mirror but face to face)[40]—for all these reasons, it would be much worse than death for him to leave the hermitage or his order, no matter who he is—whether a glorious contemplative or a simple lover.[41] Let no one be vexed with me for saying this. It is *The Experience of Truth* that I write, for I have learned these things by feeling them directly in the spirit.[42]

---

40. 1 Cor 13:12.

41. Methley's breathless, tortured syntax reflects the intensity of his feelings.

42. *ipsa affeccione in spiritu, he[c] ipsa didici.* Cf. *The Refectory of Salvation,* chap. 32, for Methley's temptation to hold office himself "in order to be of profit to all through the melting of my soul."

25. On the efficacy of divine love, which teaches everything that is needful

Some people might want to ask me more, if they had the opportunity, because love is so efficacious in every need that without error, it can teach everything that pertains to this matter.[43] Because of its sweetness in the sight of the Beloved, or rather because of the Beloved himself, love should count everything vile, even the most delightful and precious things. As I say, some would like to ask me how to attain divine love. This is surely a question no mortal can answer, unless I'm mistaken, except one who has experienced it, or at least read about it in divine scriptures.[44] To deny that one knows, I am convinced, is a lie and a falsehood—not to mention ingratitude—if a person who has this gift is asked about the love of God who gave it. Moreover, I would be in danger of withholding my talent, when I ought instead to double it with a pious intention by devoting it to the investigation of these things.[45] Let them say what I know from my own experience to be true, thanks to God: he cannot cheat his lovers of their desires, for they are always of one will. Because God has given me grace to ask for this gift, as well as the peace that belongs to his elect, I will thank him for his benefits, and seek grace in conferring benefits, with a Hail Mary— the most efficacious prayer in things of this kind.

26. What should be done to obtain some kind of perceptible love of God at all times

First of all, believe that there is a certain way of living in the present life that enjoys continual divine love. This belief is the

43. Cf. 1 John 2:27.

44. *in scripturis vbilibet diuinis.* The phrase may refer either to the Bible or to contemplative writings such as Methley's.

45. Cf. Matt 25:14-30 (the parable of the talents). Methley makes a clear distinction between preaching (rejected for Carthusians in chap. 24) and giving instruction on the contemplative life.

first virtue for seeking and finding love. Hence Scripture says, "Her conversation has no bitterness, nor her company tedium, but joy and gladness."[46]

Second, believe that it is fitting for God's faithful to preserve their state in sobriety and ascend higher by his inspiration.[47] For no one will be crowned who has not legitimately contended.[48]

Third, believe that without the gift of grace and the merit of Christ's passion, no mortal could, can, or ever would be able to satisfy God, even if he were to live for endless ages.

Fourth, believe that sin is by no means permitted, whether the sin is a spiritual or a bodily action.

Fifth, believe that a person who desires perceptible divine love must never admit human love, nor succumb to ennui.

Sixth, believe that if you resist the first stirrings of temptation, you will quickly attain perfection.

Seventh, believe that you may by no means will either to live or to be released from this body except in accord with the will of God.[49]

See, now I have said what you should do if you wish always to have some kind of perceptible love. But it will not always be to the same degree, for this is not possible.

27. On understanding the previous chapters; why revelations are given; and on virginity

Now, sweetest and most blessed fathers, brothers, and sisters,[50] know that if you wish to obtain understanding of the aforesaid

46. Wis 8:16, speaking of divine Wisdom.

47. Luke 14:10.

48. 2 Tim 2:5.

49. Phil 1:23-24. The struggle to achieve this equanimity is a major theme of *The Bedroom of the beloved Beloved*.

50. This is the only reference to "sisters" in all of Methley's extant works. There were no Carthusian nuns in England, so this unique chapter on virginity uniquely envisages an audience beyond the order or on the Continent.

things, you must ask it of God, who gives to all in abundance and without reproach, and wisdom will be given to you.[51] For sometimes God gives revelations of heavenly things to confirm the hearts of the wavering or rouse the hearts of the lukewarm. Yet a person who neither has nor understands heavenly revelations should labor with a devout intention—and by love, that person possesses the heavenly kingdom as a most chaste virgin, even if he or she is corrupt in body. But no such man or woman, I declare, will receive the crown of virgins.[52] For God can make virgins out of prostitutes,[53] just as on the contrary, men make non-virgins out of virgins. Therefore it is better to regain virginity in this way than to lose it in both ways. Incorruption makes a person close to God,[54] and whoever clings to God in love is one spirit with him.[55] And because nothing defiled enters into God,[56] such a person who is [one spirit with him] is in a way incorrupt and a virgin.[57] May God, who deigned to be born of a virgin, preserve in us one or both kinds of virginity to his perpetual praise—he who lives and reigns with the Father and the Holy Spirit, God forever and ever. Amen.

51. Jas 1:5.

52. In other words, God can forgive the loss of virginity and even restore its merits, yet this special "crown" is reserved for those who have remained physically intact. Cf. Rev 14:4-5.

53. The question of God's ability to restore lost virginity was a staple in scholastic discussions of his omnipotence. Mary Magdalene, thought to have been a prostitute, heads the list of virgin saints in the Litany. Several other saints, such as Mary of Egypt and Marina/Pelagia, were also converted prostitutes.

54. Wis 6:20.

55. 1 Cor 6:17.

56. Wis 7:25.

57. *ergo qui huiusmodi est quodammodo incorruptus, et virgo est.*

To Hugh Hermit: An Epistle on Solitary Life Nowadays

To Hugh Hermit. Here begins an epistle on solitary life nowadays.

1. God Almighty, all-knowing, all-loving, in whom is all goodness, the well of mercy and grace; the glorious Trinity, one God in three persons (that is to say, the Father and the Son and the Holy Spirit): May he bless us with his gracious goodness and bring us to his bliss in heaven. Dear brother in Christ Jesus, your desire is good and holy that you should be informed according to your position as a hermit: how you should please God for his honor and for profit to yourself. May God—for his great mercy, meekness, and grace—give us both grace: me to say well, and you to do as I say to his honor and our benefit. Amen.

2. *Eripe me de inimicis meis Domine; ad te confugi; doce me facere voluntatem tuam, quia Deus meus es tu.*[1] That is to say in English, "Lord, deliver me from my enemies; to thee I have fled; teach me to do thy will, for thou art my God." These words pertain to all Christian people who ask to be delivered from their enemies physically and spiritually, and who flee from the love of the world. But these words especially pertain to you who have fled from human fellowship to God in the wilderness, that you may better

---

1. Ps 142:9-10. This verse functions as a refrain recurring at the end of each chapter, and Methley eventually abbreviates it.

learn to do his will; for he is your God, and you are to love him especially. Therefore I will, by his grace, tell you how you should ask him to be delivered from your enemies.

3. You have three principal enemies: the world, your flesh, and the evil spirit. You might flee from the world to God. But your flesh and your enemy will go with you into the wilderness. You have wondered why I say "into the wilderness" when you dwell in a fair chapel of Our Lady—blessed, worshiped, and thanked may she be! Ask no more company for conversation except her, · I pray you, and then I say that you dwell in the wilderness well. And since you have fled from all women, if you cannot flee from your own flesh, have no woman in your mind so often as her. Then I well know you will overcome your three enemies by these three virtues, that is: against your enemy, spiritual obedience; against your flesh, pure chastity; against the world, that you return not again to it, but keep poverty with a good will. And then you can well say to God Almighty, "Lord, deliver me from my enemies, for I have fled to thee; teach me to do thy will, for thou art my God." *Eripe me de inimicis meis Domine; ad te confugi; doce me facere voluntatem tuam, quia Deus meus es tu.*

4. But how should you observe obedience, chastity, and poverty? Be obedient to God Almighty according to his law, as you promised before the bishop when you committed yourself to a hermit's life, and now also be obedient to your curate, who is your spiritual father after God and has charge of your soul. Remember then every morning and evening what you are bound to do, and thank God who has called you to it, and ask him mercy for all that you have not kept well, and say to him thus: *Eripe me de inimicis meis Domine; ad te confugi; doce me facere voluntatem tuam, quia Deus meus es tu.* And ask him grace to do better in times to come.

5. Also you must keep pure chastity. I know nothing other than that you do keep it. But yet I will tell you what I believe will do you good, by God's grace. If you keep pure chastity by God's grace in body and soul, truly to please God and Our Lady as well, there is no virtue that will bring you so soon to the true feeling of the love of God on earth. But how should you keep chastity perfectly by grace? Flee all women's fellowship, and also put the thought of them out of your mind as soon as it occurs to you, and rise up in your thought, in your heart, and in your words to God in heaven, and say thus: Jesu Jesu Jesu! *Eripe me de inimicis meis Domine; ad te confugi; doce me facere voluntatem tuam, quia Deus meus es tu.*

6. And I would have you know that there is no way that is lawful for you to enjoy the lust of the flesh. And think well on how I say "no way": neither little, nor great, nor one way, nor another. And therefore I will now tell you a remedy, and I pray you keep it well. Your thought cannot always be pure unless it is in heaven with God and Our Lady, or with some other good saint or angel. If your thought is there with love, fear, reverence, and meekness—then you dwell there, as Saint Paul says: *Nostra conversacio in celis est.*[2] "Our living is in heaven." And I pray you love well our blessed Lady and let her be your love, and say to her thus: *Tota pulchra es amica mea et macula non est in te.*[3] "All fair thou art, O my love, and there is not one spot in thee." And pray to her and send your prayers to God through her and say thus: *Eripe me de inimicis meis Domine; ad te confugi; doce me, etc.*

7. Against the riches of the world, willing poverty is a good remedy. And it is called willing poverty because it must be with a good will, and it would be full of good will if you keep it perfectly. But how should you come to this good will? By the love of God, for Scripture says this: *Si dederit homo omnem substanciam domus sue pro dileccione quasi [nihil] despiciet eam.*[4] "If a man has given all the riches of his house for the love of God, he should despise it as if it were nothing." And I say, if you once felt in your heart the love of God, you would despise all the world— not despising the creatures of God but thinking: in comparison to

2. Phil 3:20.
3. Song 4:7.
4. Song 8:7.

the love of God, all the world is but vanity.[5] And therefore when you are tempted to have worldly goods, at the first beginning of the thought, tarry no longer but say to God thus (in either English or Latin, whichever gives you more devotion): *Eripe me de inimicis meis Domine*, etc. And I will teach you to understand this verse well: *O Domine*, "O Lord"; *eripe*, "deliver"; *me*, "me"; *de inimicis meis*, "from my enemies"; *confugi*, "I have fled altogether"; *ad te*, "to thee"; *doce me*, "teach me"; *facere voluntatem tuam*, "to do thy will"; *quia Deus meus es tu*, "because thou art my God."

8. Three other things are needful for you to guard well: one is your sight, another your cell, the third is your silence, that is, hold your tongue well. Your sight must be kept well from vanities, if you expect to come to heaven's bliss. For the prophet Jeremiah says this: *Oculus meus depredatus est animam meam.*[6] "Mine eye hath preyed on my soul." That is to say: My eye has seized my soul like a prey, like thieves who lie in the wayside to rob men and await their prey when anyone passes by. So when you should be thinking of goodness—that is, of God and heavenly or wholesome things for your soul—your eye will ravish your mind here and there, unless you guard it well. And as often as you sin thereby, so often you rob your soul like a robber on the highway. And just as great as the sin is, so great a virtue you take away from your soul, and so great a blow you give your soul. And know well that no sin is small except in comparison with a greater one. It is no little thing to offend God Almighty. And have no doubt: you will have great strife with yourself before you can overcome your sight. But ask God for mercy, health, and grace, and say to him thus: *Eripe me de inimicis meis*, etc.

9. Your cell is the second thing that I mentioned. What do I call your cell, do you think, except the place of the chapel of our blessed Lady where you dwell? And you should well know that

---

5. Echoing Eccl 1:2, also a theme in *The Refectory of Salvation*.
6. Lam 3:51.

you have great reason to keep it well, because you dare not run here and there to seek your living. God has provided for you, and therefore keep to your cell, and it will keep you from sin. Be no runabout in order to see marvels, no vagabond from town to town, no wanderer waving in the wind like a skylark. But keep to your cell, and it will keep you. But now you say, perhaps you might not be able to keep to your cell, for you are sent to visit nobles in the country, whom you dare not displease. I answer and say thus: Tell them that you have forsaken the world, and therefore—except in a time of very great need, such as a time of plague or some other great need—you may not leave your devotion. And when you help them, take care that you do it truly for the love of God, and take nothing except for your expenses.

And when you sit by yourself in the wilderness and are tired or feel tedium, say this to our Lady as Saint Godric[7] said (that holy hermit): *Sancta Maria, virgo mater Jesu Christi Nazareni, protege et adiuva tuum Hugonem, suscipe et adduc cito tecum in tuum regnum vel in Dei regnum.*[8] (He said *adiuva tuum Godricum*, but you may say *tuum Hugonem*, for your name is Hugh.) That is to say in English, "Saint Mary, maiden and mother of Jesus Christ of Nazareth, hold and keep thy Hugh, take and lead him soon with thee into thy kingdom" (or say, "into the kingdom of God"—both are good). And I counsel you: love well Saint Hugh,[9] of our order of Carthusian monks. But now you say, perhaps you

7. Saint Godric (ca. 1065–1170), a hermit at Finchale near Durham, in the north of England.

8. This prayer is quoted in early Middle English in one of Godric's Latin hagiographies; see Reginald of Durham, *Libellus de vita et miraculis S. Godrici*, ed. J. Stevenson, Surtees Society 20 (1847), 119 (as cited by Hogg, *Analecta Cartusiana* 31 [1977], 117). See also J. W. Rankin, "The Hymns of St. Godric," *PMLA* 38, no. 4 (1923): 699–711. Interestingly, Methley completely abandons the vernacular poem's meter and lyricism in his translation into Latin and back into English again.

9. Saint Hugh of Lincoln (ca. 1135/40–1200), also known as Hugh of Avalon, was prior of Witham Charterhouse, the first Carthusian house in England, and responsible for its early development and success. He was later made bishop of Lincoln.

must come out to hear Mass. That seems well enough, unless you could have Masses sung in your chapel. But when you have heard Mass, then flee home, unless you have a very good cause, as you say in this verse: *Ad te confugi*; To thee, Lord, I have fled wholly, both body and soul, as thou art my all. For if you flee from the world with your body and not with your heart, then you are a false hypocrite, as Scripture says: *Simulatores et callidi provocant iram Dei.*[10] That is in English, "False wily dissemblers provoke the wrath of God." Therefore in your need to resist such temptations, say this verse: *Eripe me de inimicis meis*, etc.

10. The third thing is your silence. And know this well: it will do you great good if you think thus in your heart, making no vow unless you wish: "Good Lord, by thy grace I think this day to guard well my tongue, to your honor and my well-being." And especially on fasting days I counsel you, keep your silence and speak with no creature if you can avoid it. I have known some holy people that preserve silence on Friday, on Wednesday, or on great saints' vigils. And the prophet David says this: *Obmutui & humiliatus sum, & silui a bonis.*[11] "I have held my tongue and I have been humbled, and I have kept myself silent from good speech." Note well what he says: from good things or from good speech, I have kept myself silent. And why? For fear that even in good speech, some evil can occur. For know well, you cannot speak much good speech without some of it being empty or bad. *And on the day of judgment every man must give account of every idle word that he speaks.*[12] And therefore avoid speech. And when you feel yourself tempted to speak, say this verse: *Eripe me, Domine, etc.*

11. Now you might ask me how you should be occupied day and night. I say, with your duty that you are bound to, and then with anything more that you add to it yourself by grace and your

10. Job 36:13.
11. Ps 38:3.
12. Matt 12:36.

own devotion. Five things are appropriate for you: good prayer; meditation, which is called holy thinking; reading of holy English books; contemplation, which you may attain by means of grace and great devotion, that is, to forget all manner of things except God, and for great love of him to be rapt into contemplation; and good deeds with your hands. And I pray you, do your own chores yourself if you can, and when you are tempted to have workmen where there is no need for them, say the aforesaid verse: *Eripe me, etc.*

12. What I say now, I pray you give good heed. Scripture says thus: *Non enim habet amaritudinem conversacio illius nec tedium conuictus illius, sed leticiam & gaudium.*[13] Understand it in this way: this mode of life, that is, the holy living of a good man, has no bitterness in heart nor reluctance to live with God, but gladness and joy. So if you want to live always in joy, keep your thought always on God, with love and fear and other virtues. And in the morning and evening use long prayers or other spiritual exercises like meditation, as I said before, and other similar things. Between morning and evening say many prayers or spiritual exercises, but briefly and often. And work between them, and during the time of your work let your mind never depart from God. And in the beginning you will feel some penance or pain, but ever after you will live like a song thrush or a nightingale for joy; and thank God and pray for me, and as often as you have need say the aforesaid verse: *Eripe me, etc.*

Deo gracias Amen. Quod Ricardus Methley de Monte gracie ordinis carthusiensis fratri Hugoni deuoto heremite. [Thanks be to God, Amen. Written by Richard Methley of Mount Grace, brother of the Carthusian Order, for brother Hugh the devout hermit.]

---

13. Wis 8:16. "Her companionship has no bitterness, nor her company tedium, but joy and gladness."

Index